The Purpose-Driven University

The Purpose-Driven University: Transforming Lives and Creating Impact Through Higher Education

BY
DEBBIE HASKI-LEVENTHAL
Macquarie University, Australia

United Kingdom – North America – Japan – India – Malaysia – China

Emerald Publishing Limited
Howard House, Wagon Lane, Bingley BD16 1WA, UK

First edition 2020

© 2020 Debbie Haski-Leventhal
Published under exclusive licence by Emerald Publishing Limited

Reprints and permissions service
Contact: permissions@emeraldinsight.com

No part of this book may be reproduced, stored in a retrieval system, transmitted in any form or by any means electronic, mechanical, photocopying, recording or otherwise without either the prior written permission of the publisher or a licence permitting restricted copying issued in the UK by The Copyright Licensing Agency and in the USA by The Copyright Clearance Center. Any opinions expressed in the chapters are those of the authors. Whilst Emerald makes every effort to ensure the quality and accuracy of its content, Emerald makes no representation implied or otherwise, as to the chapters' suitability and application and disclaims any warranties, express or implied, to their use.

British Library Cataloguing in Publication Data
A catalogue record for this book is available from the British Library

ISBN: 978-1-83867-286-7 (Print)
ISBN: 978-1-83867-283-6 (Online)
ISBN: 978-1-83867-285-0 (Epub)

INVESTOR IN PEOPLE

*To Emily and Ella, my beautiful girls, who make the journey
towards purpose even more purposeful*

*To the thousands of students whom I have had the privilege
to teach and learn from*

*To all the change-makers in universities who strive
to ignite this movement*

And

*To the little boy whom I tutored all these years ago and who
made me understand what a meaningful life can look like*

Table of Contents

About the Author		*xi*
Acknowledgements		*xiii*
Introduction: The Time for Purpose Is Now		*1*
	About this Book	*5*
Chapter 1	**On Purpose, Impact, Vision and Mission**	*7*
	Changing Lives and Changing the World at Stanford University	*7*
	Introduction: The Journey towards Purpose	*8*
	Personal, Role, Organisational and Societal Purpose	*9*
	Layers of Purpose	*12*
	The Purpose-Driven University	*14*
	Between Purpose, Mission, Vision and Values	*16*
	Mission and Vision	*17*
	Values	*19*
	Imperative Questions to Ask	*20*
Chapter 2	**The Multi-level Benefits of a Strong Purpose**	*23*
	The Benefits of Purpose at Erasmus University, the Netherlands	*23*
	Introduction	*25*
	Micro-level Benefits: Changing People's Lives	*26*
	Meso-level Benefits: Helping the Organisation to Thrive	*28*
	Macro-level Benefits: Impacting Society and the Community	*30*
	Imperative Questions to Ask	*31*

Chapter 3 Responsibility, Ethics and Sustainability in Higher Education Institutions: A Holistic Approach — 35

Simon Fraser University: Leading Sustainability in a Whole-of-the-Community Engaging Way — 35
Introduction — 36
Socially Responsible Universities — 36
Ethics in Higher Education — 38
Conscious Universities — 40
Sustainable Universities — 40
    The Sustainable Development Goals — 42
The Holistic Approach to a Purpose-Driven University — 45
    Impactful Research — 46
    Purpose-Driven Teaching — 47
    Genuine Service, Engagement and Citizenship — 48
    Impact-based Promotion — 49
Imperative Questions to Ask — 50

Chapter 4 Leading Universities towards Purpose: The Role of University Leadership — 53

President Amy Gutmann: Leading Penn towards Impact — 53
Introduction — 54
Effective University Leadership — 55
Purpose-Driven Leadership — 56
Leading with Purpose, Transforming with Vision — 57
In the Service of Others — 58
High Levels of Consciousness — 60
Shared Leadership — 62
Imperative Questions to Ask — 63

Chapter 5 Purpose-related Stakeholders — 67

The Stakeholder Approach at Oxford University — 67
Stakeholder Theory and Purpose-related Stakeholders — 68
Students: The Most Purpose-Driven Generation — 71
    How to Involve Students in Purpose and Impact — 73
    Graduate Capabilities and Attributes — 74
Academic Staff — 75
Professional Staff — 77

	Other Important Stakeholders	79
	Corporate Partners	79
	Government	82
	Philanthropic Partners	83
	Environment and Community	84
	Imperative Questions to Ask	85
Chapter 6	**Measuring Impact and Storytelling**	89
	Sharing Stories of Impact at the University of Technology Sydney	89
	Introduction	91
	Measuring and Sharing the Social Impact	91
	Social Impact Tools	92
	Social Impact Measurement Guide	94
	Creating a Shared Narrative of Purpose	95
	Sharing a Story of Purpose: A New Era in Marketing	97
	Addressing Related Issues and Risks	99
	Imperative Questions to Ask	100
Chapter 7	**Leading the Change**	103
	Changing towards Purpose at the University of Auckland	103
	Introduction	105
	Organisational Change	106
	Appreciative Inquiry	107
	Kotter's Eight Steps for Organisational Change	110
	The Six Insights towards Sustainability (and Purpose)	111
	Eight Steps for Creating a Purpose-Driven Organisation	113
	Purpose Enablers	114
	Imperative Questions to Ask	115
Chapter 8	**The Purpose-Driven University Model: Six Steps for Holistic Implementation**	119
	Introduction	119
	Building Alliances	121
	Weaving Connections	122
	Rediscovering Purpose	123
	Holistic Implementation	125

		Holistic Purpose Implementation: List of Possible Initiatives	125
		Purpose-Driven Teaching	125
		Impactful Research	126
		Stakeholder Integration	126
		Environmental Sustainability	127
		Social Responsibility and Ethics	127
	Leading Impact		128
	Sharing		129
	Imperative Questions to Ask		130
Chapter 9	**The Way Forward in Higher Education**		*133*
	Innovation and Forward-thinking at KU Leuven University		133
	Introduction		134
	The Future of Higher Education		135
		The Nature of Teaching in Higher Education	135
		Higher Education in the Digital Age	136
		Student-centred Higher Education	136
		Employability in the Era of AI	137
		Collaborations and Partnerships	137
	The Future of Purpose		138
		Holistic Approach	138
		Environmental Issues: Climate Change	139
		Innovative Ways to Communicate with and Engage Stakeholders	140
		Future of Work	141
	The Future of the Purpose-Driven University and Closing Remarks		143
Epilogue			*147*
Index			*149*

About the Author

Debbie Haski-Leventhal is a Professor of Management at Macquarie Business School, and an expert in corporate social responsibility (CSR), responsible management education and volunteerism. Together with the United Nations Principles for Responsible Management Education, she conducts studies on business students around the world and their attitudes towards responsible management. In 2011, Debbie co-wrote the United Nations State of the World Volunteerism Report. She has published over 100 papers, and her work was frequently covered by the media, including the *New York Times* and the *Financial Review*. She is the author of *Strategic CSR: Tools and Theories for Responsible Management* (SAGE, 2018) and the editor-in-chief of *Society and Business Review* (Emerald). She is a TED speaker and a public speaker on CSR and purpose.

Acknowledgements

This book was such a pleasure to write. I have been thinking, feeling and dreaming about *The Purpose-Driven University* in the last three years, and it is elevating to see it printed. It has been my passion and my personal purpose, and I am delighted to finally deliver it. I could not have done this without the support of so many people, whom I would like to thank.

First, my family. To my husband, Paul, whose amazing emotional and logistic support and encouragement help me to find the moral courage to pursue my dreams: thank you for making it all possible. To my two wonderful daughters, Emily and Ella, who inspire me more than they know and who boost my motivation to fight for a better world, for them and all future generations. To my sister, Meirav, who always believes in me and my crazy dreams.

Second, my students. I was privileged to teach corporate social responsibility and social entrepreneurship over the past few years at Macquarie University, and to meet students who are not just there to gain a degree, but also a life-changing experience. This is particularly true of my students on the Master of Social Entrepreneurship program – what a spectacular group of future change-makers you are. A special thank you goes to Kristina (Kim) Panuncialman who did a research project on sustainable universities to help with the background research for this book, and to Glyn Cryer for his comments on an early version of the book.

The idea of the purpose-driven university started three years ago when I wanted to implement it at Macquarie University. Back then, I called it the Transformational University Initiative. I took it to the then Pro-Vice-Chancellor of Learning and Teaching, Professor Sherman Young, who completely came on board to work with me. I want to thank Sherman and the entire advisory board who helped to shape some of the ideas that are shared in this book: Professor Richie Howitt, Dr Kath McLachlan, Leanne Denby and JoAnne Sparks. Thank you for supporting the dream.

I would like to express my deep gratitude to all the outstanding academic leaders who, despite their busy schedule, met me and interviewed for this book. University chancellors, vice chancellors, presidents, vice presidents, social impact leaders, professors, students and others: your insights and enthusiasm informed and inspired.

I would also like to thank my many colleagues who were excited by this book and who shared ideas with me on purpose-driven universities. Special gratitude to

Professor Jennifer Leigh: you are such an inspirational and kind woman, and to Dr Lonneke Roza, it is a pleasure working with you for the last decade.

I would like to thank Macquarie University and the Dean of Macquarie University Business School, Professor Stephen Brammer, who encouraged me to pursue the idea of the purpose-driven university. It is delightful to work with a dean who is so purpose-driven.

Finally, I would like to express my gratitude to the team at Emerald Publishing and to Kimberley Chadwick, Senior Commissioning Editor, who worked with me through this process and shared my enthusiasm. I would also like to thank Sharon Cawood for proofreading the book.

Introduction: The Time for Purpose Is Now*

What is the purpose of universities, and what is their role in our world? Many would say that it is to educate students and conduct research. This is true, but somehow, the narrow focus on these two goals led universities to be perceived as ivory towers and detached elitist institutions. Many universities still focus too narrowly on ranking, profits and graduate income, instead of on real societal impact. An increasing number of graduates are now saying that their education was a waste of time and money (Hall, 2019). I have recently discovered the top Google search results for 'Universities are' (Fig. I.1).

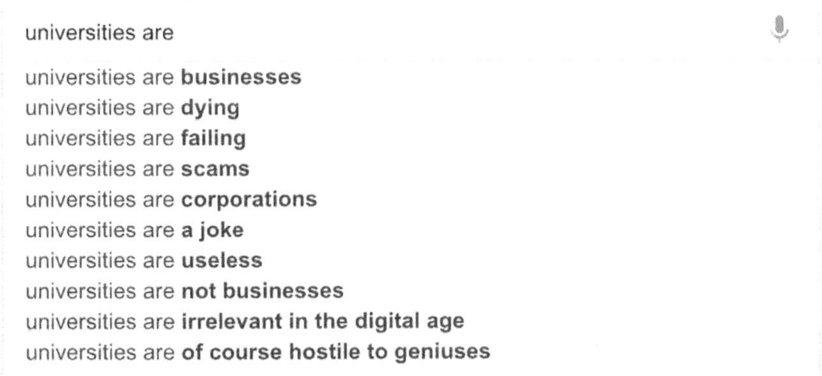

universities are

universities are **businesses**
universities are **dying**
universities are **failing**
universities are **scams**
universities are **corporations**
universities are **a joke**
universities are **useless**
universities are **not businesses**
universities are **irrelevant in the digital age**
universities are **of course hostile to geniuses**

Fig. I.1. Top Google Search Results for 'Universities are', November 2018.

The results in Fig. I.1 are very revealing. To me, these results indicate a broken system, something that needs to change profoundly and urgently. No university wants to be failing, a scam and, of course, hostile to geniuses. How did we get to

---

*Part of this introduction was presented in my TEDx talk 'The Purpose-Driven University': www.ted.com/talks/debbie_haski_leventhal_the_purpose_driven_university.

this situation? The recent admissions scandal in the USA; alleged academic leadership corruption in several universities in the last few years elsewhere; caring more about impact factors than real social impact and about how much our graduates make instead of the impact that they can make, are all factors that have led to these negative results. What we need are universities that are impactful and purposeful and that reconnect with the community. What we need are purpose-driven universities.

My personal journey towards the idea of the purpose-driven university started when I was 20. I left my home in Tel Aviv to study philosophy at the Hebrew University in Jerusalem. I came from a family in which my mother only had 10 years of schooling, and her mother was never allowed to go to school and was illiterate. I was the first person in my entire family, including my many cousins, to go to university and my parents could not understand why it was so important for me to obtain higher education, particularly studying something as 'impractical' as philosophy. Not only did I not have their emotional support, but I had no financial support either. For the three years of my first degree, I often went through the day hungry, as I had no money to support myself. To manage financially, I took on some odd student jobs. In an entrepreneurial spirit, I spread ads all around the campus and started typing students' assignments, as back in those days not every student had a laptop. What I did next changed my life.

I joined a student tutoring project, *PERACH* (an acronym for a tutoring project in Hebrew, meaning 'flower'). Similar to Big-Brother-Big-Sister, PERACH is an Israeli not-for-profit organisation which involves tens of thousands of university students each year in mentoring and assisting children, usually from disadvantaged families. For this work, the students receive enough to cover nearly half their university tuition fees. I desperately needed the financial assistance, so I committed to working with an 8-year-old boy for a year, spending four hours a week teaching him and helping him through his struggles. He was sweet and talented but a little 'nerdy' and he was bullied. His teacher told me she was anxious about his future, something that stayed with me for years. I often wondered what happened to him.

I felt that I made a difference in this boy's life and I was emotionally engaged with this work, so I ended up volunteering for another year, to later become a volunteer coordinator, managing 40 volunteers, and in the following year 60 students. At the age of 24, I became the vice-manageress of the entire project in Jerusalem, in charge of over 50 coordinators, 1000 students and the children with whom they worked. Although I was determined to be a writer since the age of 8, after finding my purpose and passion I decided to change my career path, studied a Master of Management of Not-for-profit Organisations and later wrote a PhD on volunteering. My first degree was important, and while much of it remains with me until this very day, it was the extra-curricular volunteering that changed my life. It helped me to develop a meaningful career, leading, nowadays, to being a professor of corporate social responsibility and volunteering.

After finishing my PhD on the organisational socialisation of volunteers, I published many papers on the pro-social behaviour of individuals and co-wrote the United Nations State of the World Volunteerism Report in 2011. During these years, I also started taking a great interest in the pro-social behaviour of companies. I learned that many large multinational corporations have been irresponsible, focusing mainly on short-term profits and harming humans, animals and our planet. However, at the same time, there were many companies that were using the power of business as a force for good, companies such as Patagonia, an apparel company that cares so much about the environment that it tells people not to buy its products; and Ben & Jerry's, a leading ice-cream company with a robust set of values which uses its brand to fight for what is right – 'we are a company with a social mission, we just happen to make ice-cream'. I have also seen CEOs like Paul Polman of Unilever completely changing the direction of a large multinational corporation towards sustainability and positive impact.

In my book, *Strategic Corporate Social Responsibility: Tools and Theories for Responsible Management* (2018), I used these inspirational examples and discussed this shift. I discovered that when companies genuinely focus on the positive impact they can create in the world, they attract talent, engage their employees, create consumer loyalty and enhance their reputation in the community. The global issues that we currently face cannot be addressed by governments alone, and business has an incredible power to be a force for good. Why cannot universities do the same?

If I could work anywhere, I would work for a company that is strongly led by purpose. However, I am an academic – I worked hard to become a professor, and I love what I do. Subsequently, three years ago, I started asking myself 'what if...?'. What if universities can be as purpose-driven as Patagonia and Ben & Jerry's? What if universities used their power, resources, people, incredible intellect and even their physical campuses to create a positive impact in the world? I wanted to discover the unique impact purpose of my own university and that of other universities, in order to play with the idea that universities are, or can become, a force for good. I worked with others to discuss these ideas and further develop them.

On diving into this, I discovered an emerging movement. While many universities around the globe are still obsessed with ranking and excellence and being 'the best in the world', a growing number of universities care about being 'the best *for* the world'. Stanford University is using its incredible research capabilities for social innovation and impact and to fight poverty. The University of Auckland is devoting itself to the Sustainable Development Goals, to help the world achieve these global goals by 2030. The University of Technology Sydney has an outstanding social impact framework, centred around the notion of it being an agent for social change. These and others are not only working to change the world, they are also changing the essence of higher education.

These universities lead with a strong sense of purpose: the reason for which something exists, and the reason it is done, made or used. Purpose is our reason for being, which rarely changes over time, although it may inspire and enable change. This led me to think about the reason for which universities were created and about the similarity between the words 'university' and 'universe' (defined as 'combined into one, whole'). Universities were established to create *universitas magistrorum et scholarium* – a whole community of scholars combined into one to enhance knowledge and impact the world. Furthermore, 'to educate' means to open minds and lead forth (Helfand, 2011). We have somewhat shifted away from these original purposes.

In the context of the purpose-driven university, I refer to 'impact purpose': the purpose of helping others, creating a positive impact and making a difference in someone else's life, like that little boy I tutored all these years ago. Impact purpose provides fulfilment, a sense of meaningfulness and even happiness.

As such, and as will be explained in this book, *a purpose-driven university utilises its resources, knowledge, talent and people to continuously and intentionally contribute to the communities and the environment in which it operates: through research, education, programmes and service.*

Leading with purpose is important because many universities are public organisations and/or they are using the money of students, governments or even wealthy donors, and, as such, they have a responsibility to play a role beyond providing students with degrees and conducting research. It is about *how* we educate students and how we provide them with graduate capabilities that enable them to contribute to the world. It is about measuring research impact beyond citation numbers and top-tier journals: How does this research lead to an improvement in life quality around the world? It is about caring about the impact that teaching is creating, beyond teaching evaluations.

It is not about marketing and public relations (PR) although communication and storytelling are an essential element of it. To become a purpose-driven university, a holistic approach is required, one that is embedded in every aspect of the university: from its mission statement, through its teaching and research, to managing people, profits and the planet. It is about discovering and rediscovering the purpose of each university, living by it and sharing an incredible story of change and impact. Of course, it may have a positive impact on marketing, students and staff attraction and profits, but these are not the reasons to embark on this journey.

This book is, therefore, based on the decision to share everything that I have learned through this work, together with my knowledge on corporate social responsibility, so that other universities can implement it. The goal of this book is to capture the shift towards purpose in higher education and to offer a new approach. The book offers the why, how and what of a purpose-driven university, utilising cases, research, concepts and a framework which can be implemented in any university interested in being different by genuinely making a difference. This book tells the stories of purpose-driven universities and other organisations and serves as a call for action by academic leadership.

I concluded all my interviews with purpose-driven university leaders around the world with one question: 'what other universities are doing remarkable work on purpose?' To my surprise, most interviewees could not name any other universities who are striving to create a social impact, sustainable development or stakeholder engagement. Most of the universities featured in the book are making outstanding efforts, but they do it in silos. To create a movement, it is vital to have a shared concept with other actors. Therefore, the book aims to connect all current and future purpose-driven universities, provide them with a common name and definition, and demonstrate what is happening outside the campus of each university.

The time for the purpose-driven university movement is now. Businesses have been focusing on increasing engagement around purpose for the last 20 years, but many universities still stand by educating students and conducting research as their sole purpose. However, teaching and research are their 'what', not their 'why'. If we continue down this path, we expose ourselves to more criticism and scrutiny, and we may lose even more legitimacy. We can change public perception of higher education by asking ourselves: Why do we teach? Why do we conduct research? And how can both become more impactful and meaningful?

About this Book

The book has nine chapters. It begins by examining what purpose is, the different layers of purpose and the differences between purpose, mission, vision and values to define the concept of a purpose-driven university. The second chapter details the multi-level benefits of a purpose-driven organisation for people, the organisation and society, to present a rationale, or a 'business case', for changing an organisation into a purpose-driven one. The following chapter, Chapter 3, applies knowledge from corporate social responsibility, ethics, conscious capitalism and sustainability to offer a holistic approach to the purpose-driven university. Chapter 4 discusses the prominence of responsible, ethical and conscious leadership in the context of higher education. This is followed by Chapter 5 which focuses on the purpose-related stakeholders of any university, from students and staff to government and donors. It discusses the impact of stakeholder integration as a new approach to working with and involving all the university's stakeholders in this shift towards an impact purpose. Chapter 6 examines the ways in which universities can create, measure and communicate their social impact, and how storytelling is becoming such a core component of purpose-driven marketing. For those universities that desire to implement all these ideas, Chapter 7 sheds light on organisational changes and presents inspirational frameworks, such as The Appreciative Inquiry, to lead the charge towards purpose. Chapter 8 is central to the whole book, as it presents the purpose-driven university framework – a step-by-step guide to implementing everything discussed in the book and creating a purpose-driven university. Finally, Chapter 9 considers the way forward – the future of higher education, the future of purpose and the future of the purpose-driven university – to end the book with some concluding thoughts.

Each chapter begins with an inspirational case study of a university that exemplifies the aspects of that chapter. None of these universities is perfect or flawless, but they do lead the way in some aspect of a purpose-driven organisation. As per my book on corporate social responsibility, it was an intentional decision to focus on the positive examples which can inspire change and action, and not on the scandals or unethical behaviour. We can learn more from positive illustrations that pave the way, than from negative examples which do not leave us with solutions.

Each chapter also includes many other cases and examples, related ideas and concepts, research and frameworks. The book is based on numerous interviews with university leaders, academic staff, students and others, as well as on a document analysis of public reports and universities' websites. It also presents examples of businesses and social enterprises where these are relevant and applicable to higher education. To avoid over referencing, most of these examples have one or two links to their websites, as most of this information is publicly available.

The book was mainly written for university leaders: presidents and vice presidents; chancellors, vice chancellors and deputy vice chancellors; and deans and deputy deans. However, by university leaders, we also refer to informal leaders – from academic staff who care deeply about the purpose of the university to professional staff who can be the heroes of implementation. It also includes the millions of students who are purpose-driven and would like to revolutionise higher education, so it becomes more purposeful and meaningful – to them and others. Let the revolution of purpose in higher education begin.

References

Hall, J. (2019). *My $110,000 degree was a waste of time and money*. Retrieved from www.news.com.au/finance/work/careers/my-110000-degree-was-a-waste-of-time-and-money/news-story/2260ece62e5f63208f9cc187e1294c9e

Haski-Leventhal, D. (2018). *Strategic corporate social responsibility: Tools and theories for responsible management*. London: SAGE.

Helfand, D. (2011). Higher education: Academic questions. *Nature*, *477*(7363), 158.

Chapter 1

On Purpose, Impact, Vision and Mission

Changing Lives and Changing the World at Stanford University

Founded in 1885 by California senator Leland Stanford and his wife, Jane, Stanford is an American private research university, known for its academic excellence, its ability to raise large funds and its connection to Silicon Valley. Ranked as one of the world's top universities, Stanford University comprises seven schools and 18 interdisciplinary institutes, with more than 16,000 students, 2100 faculty and 1800 postdoctoral scholars. It is one of the most sought-after universities in the USA, leading to very low acceptance rates in student admissions. As of October 2018, 83 Nobel laureates, 27 Turing Award laureates and eight Fields Medallists have been affiliated with Stanford as students, alumni, faculty or staff. Its annual research budget in 2016 was a staggering US$1.6 billion (Stanford, 2019).

However, Stanford was not always this successful. After the death of its founder only a few years after it was founded, the University struggled financially. It also had difficulties following the extensive damage caused to it by the 1906 and the 1989 San Francisco earthquakes. Stanford University became the success story that it is today by leading academic, research and teaching excellence; by holding a close relationship with Silicon Valley; and by becoming a purpose-driven university. Stanford leads with this mission statement:

> To promote the public welfare by exercising an influence on behalf of humanity and civilization, teaching the blessings of liberty regulated by law, and inculcating love and reverence for the great principles of government as derived from the inalienable rights of man to life, liberty, and the pursuit of happiness.

As such, Stanford aims to create a large-scale impact on humanity and global society. Its core values are: Ethics – to anchor education and research in ethics and human welfare; Boldness – to advance its mission boldly but with an eagerness to collaborate and learn from others; and Foundations – to stay true to its values, including integrity, diversity, respect, freedom of inquiry and expression, tenacity and optimism. Stanford's current president, Marc Tessier-Lavigne, introduced the IDEAL (Inclusion, Diversity, Equity and Access in a Learning community) Initiative to achieve a purpose, mission and values for the 'betterment of humanity'.

Stanford University is known for its experiential and impactful learning. One of its outstanding examples is 'The Alternative Breaks @ Stanford Program', which exposes students to complex social and cultural issues through community visits, experiential learning, direct service, group discussion and reflection. The purpose of this programme is to transform students into advocates of social change on issues affecting local communities. In 2019, the programme offered courses such as 'Saving the World? Exploring the Ethics of International Service and Aid', 'Design Thinking for Social Innovation' and 'Capital or Community: Housing Inequality in the Bay Area'. In addition, students can participate in 'Impact Abroad', an international volunteering programme in which students are involved in a 'meaningful and enriching' project in developing nations.

The University leads research centres and schools aimed at creating a social impact. For example, Stanford's *Center for Social Innovation* educates future leaders about social and environmental change in order to strengthen the capacity of individuals and organisations to develop innovative solutions to complex problems. Stanford Graduate School of Business aims to 'Change lives. Change organizations. Change the world'. Its *Corporations and Society Initiative* explores the interactions between private and public sector institutions and the rest of society. Moreover, the *Stanford Center on Poverty and Inequality* is committed to providing research, policy analysis and training on issues of poverty and inequality.

With its strong purpose, mission statement, values, impactful curriculum, experiential learning, research centres and collaboration with all sectors of the economy, Stanford University shows that a university can leverage its resources, knowledge, talent and power to make a positive impact on society and the world.

Introduction: The Journey towards Purpose

Three people were crushing rocks side by side on a construction site. Another person walked by and asked each of them what their job is. The first person answered, 'My job is to do what I am told for eight hours a day so I can get paid'. The second person replied, 'My job is to crush rocks'. The third person said, 'My job is to build a cathedral'. The cathedral is not only the third person's job, but a motivator, a sense of being part of something greater than ourselves, and a purpose.

Purpose is the new black. Books and media on purpose, such as *Start with Why* (Sinek, 2011), *The Purpose Driven Life* (Warren, 2002) and *Conscious Capitalism* (Mackey & Sisodia, 2014), are gaining popularity. People, particularly millennials, are looking to live a meaningful life and have a meaningful job. Purpose-driven organisations can offer this to help create motivation, engagement and impact. After decades of being told that happiness will be brought by consumerism, people have begun to discover that consumption provides only a short-term pleasure – not happiness – and that it can also have devastating negative impacts on this planet and its inhabitants. Some people try to find meaning through other channels, such as religion or volunteering, but these do not work for everyone.

Subsequently, many are searching for their life purpose or for a purpose-driven organisation to work for or engage with, in order to find meaning and happiness. Research (e.g. Schwartz & Porath, 2014) has found that when people work for a purpose-driven organisation, there is a spill-over effect, and they start to share a sense of purpose. Consequently, numerous companies have started to define their purpose, communicate it to employees and consumers and recognise leaders who act from a higher purpose. Purpose-driven marketing and storytelling are now used to enhance the reputation of organisations and to create an emotional connection to a brand and its product line.

This journey towards purpose, social responsibility and sustainability did not entirely skip the higher education sector. However, it does not seem to be in the advanced stages seen in the corporate sector. A global movement is emerging, with an increasing number of universities focusing on their social impact and environmental footprint. Some universities are changing their vision and mission statement to capture this shift. There are remarkable efforts in using innovative solutions and education to create a positive impact in the world, and these will be featured in the book.

There are negative public perceptions about universities – that they are elitist, tax-exempt institutions, obsessed with making profits; that they are detached ivory towers that are not contributing enough to society. In the USA, higher education in leading universities can be so expensive that universities play a role in social immobility. Of course, there are also positive perceptions of the role universities play in, for example, conducting life-changing medical research and the advancement of knowledge.

The key to overcoming negative perceptions and to enhancing positive views is having a strong purpose, a profound commitment to this purpose and the embeddedness of this purpose in every decision and action. Positive public perceptions are important as they may translate into government funding, corporate support, alumni pride and giving, young people's desire to gain an education and their family's encouragement to do so.

The aim of this chapter is to illustrate how universities can better communicate their purpose to become the destination of choice for purpose-driven students and staff. It begins with differentiating between personal, organisational and societal purpose and categorising impact, relational and integrated purposes. The concept of the purpose-driven university is then presented and defined. This is followed by a discussion of the differences and connections between purpose, vision, mission and values.

Personal, Role, Organisational and Societal Purpose

According to the dictionary definition (Cambridge Dictionary, 2019), a purpose is a reason for which something exists or is done, made or used. A personal purpose is usually defined by an individual based on values, life goals and the meaning attached to life. The meaning of life has occupied people since the dawn of humanity, given our individual, short existence on this planet. One way of addressing this search for meaning is by having a well-defined personal purpose. This purpose can range from taking care of our family to combatting cancer. A purposeful life can provide meaningfulness and even happiness (Robak & Griffin, 2000). Some people use their religion to define their life purpose, while others find other sources for it, such as family, work, skills and passion. Pink (2009) defines purpose as the sense that what we do produces something transcendent or serves something meaningful beyond ourselves. It refers to the desire to do something important that has meaning, usually with the focus on a 'bigger picture', something more important than just one's own interests.

According to Mackey and Sisodia (2014), a purpose is a definitive statement about the difference that a person is trying to make. It is not what a person does (a job), but what he or she stands for. A purpose is most powerful when it taps into a universal truth, aligning with the higher aspects of what it means to be human. As explained by Christensen (2017), a purpose is about what a person wants to achieve in the far future for themselves or for others.

Many people define their life purpose in terms of the work that they do, which is their **role purpose**. A medical doctor can define her purpose as saving people's lives. A teacher may feel that his life purpose is to raise a new generation of curious children. A gardener can define her life purpose in cultivating the environment and improving people's joy and quality of life. Often, life purpose and work purpose meet in professions in which one helps others to improve their lives. However, anyone can find meaning in their work by discovering how they can help others or connect to a collective purpose, such as an organisational or societal purpose.

Like people, organisations can also have a purpose, an **organisational purpose**. The very definition of an organisation is a group of people working interdependently to achieve a common goal. As such, every organisation should have a purpose. However, for it to impart meaning, this purpose needs to move beyond the products or services an organisation creates or provides to the impact and value it helps to create.

In a study conducted by EY (2015, p. 1), organisational purpose was defined as 'an aspirational reason for being which inspires and provides a call to action for an organisation and its partners and stakeholders and provides benefit to local and global society'. It is the organisational reason for being, which rarely changes over time, although it may inspire and enable change. According to Hemerling, White, Swan, Castellana Kreisman, and Reed (2018), purpose is the organisation's 'why', as it articulates why its work matters to the world. Purpose is the foundation on which the organisation's mission, vision, values and culture are built. It lies at the intersection of two fundamental questions: who we are (what our authentic and distinctive strengths are) and what human need we fulfil in society. As explained by Quinn and Thakor (2018), a higher purpose is not about economic exchange; rather, it reflects something more aspirational. It explains how the people involved with an organisation are making a difference, and, as such, purpose gives them a sense of meaning and draws their support. While corporate and other leaders can be sceptical about purpose at first, many grow to understand its importance over time. As Sinek was quoted in an *HBR* article (Hedges, 2017): 'Profit isn't a purpose. It's a result. To have purpose means the things we do are of real value to others'.

A compelling purpose reduces friction within the organisation and its ecosystem because it connects everyone and moves them in the same direction (Mackey & Sisodia, 2014). In an interview, Sisodia said that 'every decision should be looked at in terms of purpose. Some decisions may be purpose-neutral. But purpose is certainly not just a marketing issue or positioning of your brand image. Purpose should impact every aspect of the firm' (Phelps, 2017).

As such, many organisations aim to define their purpose, but some are truly purpose-led. A purpose-driven organisation is one that has a clear goal that surpasses meeting market demand in which it acknowledges the interdependence of business and society (Hollensbe, Wookey, Loughlin, George, & Nichols, 2014).

The leading purpose-driven companies emphasise their purpose, sometimes over their products. Purpose-driven companies, such as Ben & Jerry's and others, are not defined by the products or services they sell, their financial success or the power of their brand. Such companies are defined by the impact they create and the difference they make in people's lives.

Companies like Ben & Jerry's or The Body Shop were founded on a social mission and a purpose. Similarly, social enterprises are organisations that are explicitly built to serve a well-defined purpose. Such is the case of Tony Chocolonely, a Dutch Chocolate company that was founded to raise awareness of slavery and child labour in the industry. Thankyou started as a bottled water company in Australia to address inaccessibility to clean water and moved to selling other products to address other global issues.

Other companies, such as PepsiCo and Unilever, discovered their purpose in later stages of their organisational life, usually with the leadership of a new CEO. Indra Nooyi, who served as chairperson of PepsiCo and as CEO for 13 years from 2006 to 2019, coined the idea of 'performance with purpose', striving to change business so that it serves society. Unilever's CEO from 2009 to 2019, Paul Polman, developed Unilever's 'Sustainable Living Plan' to create sustainable development. It is never too late for an organisation to develop an impact purpose.

Reyes and Kleiner (1990, p. 51) argued that 'developing an organisational purpose is more an art rather than a science. Deriving a purpose requires imagination, imagery and innovation. To keep it alive, it requires commitment'. The first step in developing an organisational purpose is to build a vision and ask key questions such as: What does the organisation stand for? Where do we want to be in the industry?

In addition to organisational purpose, we should also discuss **societal purpose**. Many nations, particularly those with high levels of collectivism (as opposed to individualism), share goals which governments, institutions and individuals collaborate to achieve. To illustrate, we may consider the collective efforts of individuals and institutions in the former Soviet Union or China today. However, it is not only communist countries that have shared goals. Many countries in Northern Europe work collectively to reduce their carbon emissions and preserve

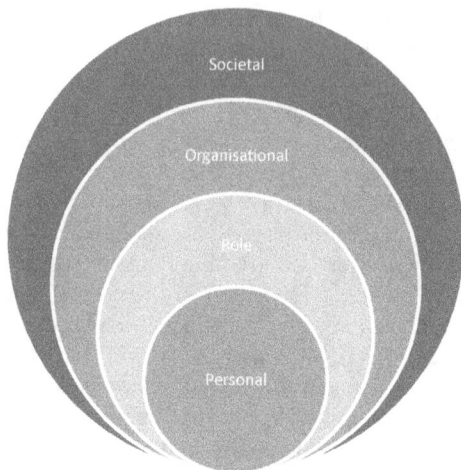

Fig. 1.1. Four Layers of Purpose.

the planet, a goal which takes many individuals and organisations to achieve. In the same vein, we can see global efforts by governments, institutions, organisations and individuals to achieve global goals, or the sustainable development goals (see Chapter 3), in a combined effort.

These four layers of purpose (Fig. 1.1), namely personal, role, organisational and societal, can exist separately. A woman might help children as her personal purpose, serve customers as her role purpose, sell products to achieve her employer's organisational purpose and contribute to the community. However, when the personal purpose aligns with the role, organisational and societal purposes, there is a sense of congruence and satisfaction, in life and at work.

A famous example of such an alignment is based on the story of President John F. Kennedy visiting NASA headquarters for the first time in 1961. While touring the facility, he introduced himself to a janitor who was mopping the floor and asked him what he did at NASA. 'I am helping to put a man on the moon!', answered the janitor, demonstrating how the organisational and social purpose became his personal and role purpose in what might be considered as a simple job.

Layers of Purpose

Another categorisation of purpose is according to impact purpose, relational purpose and integrated purpose. The first of these is particularly crucial for our discussion on the purpose-driven university.

Purpose-driven organisations often define their goals through an **impact purpose**. An impact purpose is how a person or an organisation contributes to the world beyond their normal conduct. A company's purpose goes beyond hiring people and selling products which may serve the needs of its customers. A person's purpose goes beyond family and work. And a university's purpose should reach beyond conducting research and teaching students.

Impact (also known as social impact) is the change that is made in people's lives, and it is usually defined in terms of long-term and macro-level changes. As will be explained in Chapter 6, the basic logic model differentiates between inputs (the resources we use to create this impact), activities, outputs, outcomes and impact. Impact is related to changes such as quality of life, social value, collective access to basic goods and so on.

While it is difficult to assess social impact, due to issues such as attribution and the need to run large-scale longitudinal studies, it is vital to define the positive impact as the goal a university aims to create. For example, the mission of MIT is to 'advance knowledge and educate students in science, technology, and other areas of scholarship that will best serve the nation and the world in the 21st century' (MIT, 2019). This purpose is not only to advance education and knowledge, but also to serve the nation, which is a societal purpose and a macro-level impact.

The relational purpose focuses on the organisation's relationships with internal and external stakeholders. For many business organisations, a relational purpose focuses on the relationship of the firm with consumers, employees, shareholders and others. Relationships are important to most humans and organisations, which is the reason why most motivation theories include a relational motivation (e.g. the 'belonging' need in Maslow's hierarchy or the 'need to bond' in Nohria's four needs model). Consequently, working with stakeholders can help to meet the social needs of employees and clarify the purpose of the organisation.

A well-known example from the business world of a relational purpose is the Johnson & Johnson Credo, which details the company's responsibility towards customers, doctors, employees, communities and stockholders. Similarly, the University of California, Berkeley (2019) details its mission in terms of stakeholders: '[to serve] our community, our state, our nation, and the world; to providing access for students from all backgrounds and communities; and to fostering in our students, faculty, and staff a strong ethic of public service and social justice'. It is, of course, possible to integrate impact purpose and relational purpose when discussing the impact and value that the organisation aims to create for its stakeholders.

Finally, an **integrated purpose** is imperative for purpose-driven organisations. First, an integrated purpose is embedded in everything that the organisation does. It is not the responsibility of the formal leaders alone, but a shared duty of everyone, including internal and external stakeholders. In some universities, such as the University of Technology Sydney or Simon Fraser University, a multi-stakeholder approach was used to define the purpose of the university and its desired impact, and to later achieve it. As such, the second part of an integrated purpose is what is achieved through collaboration and empowerment. Every person and stakeholder group becomes an ambassador for the purpose and the entities in charge of helping to deliver it. Finally, it is acted upon and embedded in every action that we take. An integrated purpose acts as a social glue and holds everyone accountable. In organisations with an integrated purpose, employees can question the leadership on its actions and alignment with purpose.

The Purpose-Driven University

In a world with over 10,000 universities, hundreds of millions of students and millions engaged in teaching and research, what makes a university stand out in a crowded market? Most universities share the maxim of *rerum cognoscere causas* (to know the causes of things), but what is their unique value proposition? Many universities try to address this by communicating their competitive advantage in numbers – student numbers, graduate income or funds raised. Others celebrate the success of their academic staff, with Nobel laureates or Fields Medallists, or boast about the history of the institution. However, this may not necessarily engage students, staff and external stakeholders. While everyone wants to affiliate with success stories, people are also keen to belong to organisations with which they have a strong value congruence and purpose alignment.

Alternatively, higher education institutions can utilise concepts such as organisational purpose and impact purpose to create value for individuals, the university and society at large. Defining a unique and robust impact purpose is the first step in turning an academic institution into a purpose-driven university. Gamoran (2018) argued that higher education institutions that turn their attention to serving the public good may be best poised to thrive and deliver lasting value, and, as such, some universities are embarking on innovations to support social engagement among students, and initiating university-wide efforts to educate students for social impact.

Based on the aforementioned concepts surrounding purpose, I have developed the idea of the purpose-driven university and created a working definition to inspire action:

> A purpose-driven university utilises its resources, knowledge, talent and people to continuously and intentionally contribute to the communities and the environment in which it operates: through research, education, programmes and service.

To illustrate, Stanford University (2019) defined its purpose as being 'to promote the public welfare by exercising an influence on behalf of humanity'. This is a compelling impact purpose which helps Stanford University to stand out, together with its other positive attributes. Similarly, MIT's purpose is 'to make a better world through education, research, and innovation' and the University of Edinburgh aims to 'deliver impact for society' and to 'make a significant, sustainable and socially responsible contribution to the world'.

Purpose can be defined in terms of the unique impact a university creates in people's lives. As a higher education institution, what long-lasting macro-level impact is created? Universities provide students with degrees and diplomas, but how do these students then use these degrees to benefit others? Universities lead cutting-edge research, but how does this translate into better lives around the globe? As such, to define the university's purpose, it is essential to determine and measure the social impact it creates, both directly and indirectly.

There are other notable examples which demonstrate how universities and colleges define their purpose. Boston College (BC) is a Catholic University that develops students from diverse faith backgrounds to become individuals 'in service to others'. As the leading university in the liberal arts, scientific inquiry and student formation, BC believes in 'education with a heart and soul – and the power to transform'.

Princeton University's informal motto is 'In the Nation's Service and the Service of Humanity', constantly inspiring 'Princetonians' to contribute extraordinarily to society. By providing resources and support, students and alumni are encouraged to connect their learning with service so that they can direct their research, education and lives to benefit humanity, Princeton's purpose being 'to be a public-spirited institution contributing through research, teaching, and engagement to its communities'.

The University of Melbourne is a leading higher education institution in Australia, and its engagement commitments include public value, engaged students and engaged research. Under the theme 'relationship with society', Kyoto University commits to a broad social engagement in cooperation with local and national society. Human rights, gender equality, and health, safety and environment are prioritised to achieve this purpose.

These purpose statements are excellent, but it is also essential to ensure that the purpose does not remain as nothing more than a statement. As emphasised throughout the book, a purpose needs to be embedded in everything that the university does, so that it becomes meaningful, long-lasting and impactful.

Box 1.1. Starting with Why

In his bestselling book *Start with Why*, and in one of the most-watched TED talks, Simon Sinek (2011) explains how successful leaders and organisations work. Sinek conceived the 'Golden Circle', with 'why' in the middle of it, followed by 'how' and 'what'. While most organisations and leaders know *what* they do and *how* they do it, those that truly stand out are the ones that work inside out, starting with a clear *why* or purpose. When people, companies and universities know why they do what they do, they engage everyone who shares the same values and purpose. 'People don't buy what you do, they buy why you do it', said Sinek. A strong 'why' can set an organisation apart and offer a unique value proposition and a social value proposition. A strong 'why' inspires people to act together to achieve that shared cause.

Sinek uses several examples, mainly of Apple, to illustrate the Golden Circle. Back when Sinek gave his TED talk in 2009, Apple had years of communicating its reason for being: thinking differently, making a dent in the universe and celebrating leaders who are crazy enough to think they can change the world. Everything they did was about challenging the status quo and changing the world. Apple's purpose could not be to manufacture

Box 1.1. *(Continued)*

computers, as this is what everyone in the industry does. Nor can its purpose be to make money (or maximise shareholder value), as this is the result of what they do, not their purpose. Even offering jobs and contributing to the economy are not unique. A purpose is about *why* we deliver products and services, about what makes the organisation stand out.

In the same vein, a university's purpose cannot be to generate research and educate students. This is what all universities do. What makes this university different? It is crucial to define the university's purpose in unique terms, such as public welfare, compassion and wellbeing. Stanford Business School does not only aim to teach business management or even to develop successful business leaders. Instead, it aims to change lives and change the world.

Between Purpose, Mission, Vision and Values

Fig. 1.2 shows the five levels of organisational identity: (1) founding philosophy (why the organisation was founded); (2) current purpose and goals (how the organisation is making a difference); (3) mission and vision (what the organisation wants to achieve and how); (4) values (what guide the organisation in achieving the above); and (5) actions (what the organisation is doing today). There is a difference between these five levels: founding philosophy and purpose are the reason for being which rarely changes over time. The vision is the ideal result for the organisation and the world it wants to build. A mission is a written statement that explains what the organisation does, for whom, how and why. Values are the motivational goals, which should also be strongly connected to purpose. Finally, actions speak louder than all the above, showing how the organisation achieves its purpose, mission, vision and values. Purpose activates the mission, values and actions, and the actions confirm the mission and the purpose.

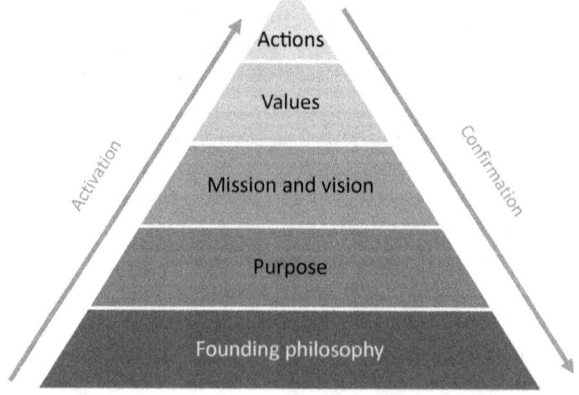

Fig. 1.2. Four Levels of Organisational Identity.

Mission and Vision

A mission statement describes the fundamental and unique purpose of an organisation and proclaims its purpose. It is not identical to purpose, but it should include the purpose as the 'why' behind what the organisation does and how. It details why an organisation exists and identifies the needs it aspires to address (Chandler, 2017). Mission statements describe the core purpose, philosophy, values and competencies of an organisation (Davis, Ruhe, Lee, & Rajadhyaksha, 2007). In doing so, a mission statement allows internal and external stakeholders to function as one and to embrace the organisational goals as their own, while providing a basis for a psychological contract between an organisation and its employees (Palmer & Short, 2008).

Higher education institutions devote considerable attention to their strategies and mission statements often because they must comply with accreditation processes, which examine the alignment between mission and performance (Palmer & Short, 2008). Indeed, mission statements are so important to higher education accreditation bodies such as the Association to Advance Collegiate Schools of Business (AACSB) that they provide very detailed guidelines on mission statements and conduct-related research.

Several studies have analysed universities' mission statements. For example, Davis et al. (2007) found that students at universities with ethical statements in their mission statements had significantly higher perceived character trait importance and character reinforcement than those at universities whose mission statements lacked ethical components. Palmer and Short (2008) analysed mission statements from 408 AACSB-accredited business schools and found that missions generally lacked comprehensiveness and that performance was rarely related to mission content.

For this book, we conducted a thorough theme analysis of the mission statements of the leading 100 universities in the world (Times Higher Education, 2018). The results show that while most of these universities had a mission statement (surprisingly, not all of them), many had disclosed no sense of purpose. Numerous mission statements focused broadly on excellence and integrity, to sound remarkably similar. However, there were a few outstanding examples, with 16% of the mission statements we looked at having 10 or more purpose-related keywords (e.g. sustainability, impact, equality, community and society).

The University of Southern California (USC, 2019) was one of these universities. Founded in 1880, USC is the oldest private research university in California. Its central mission has long been 'the development of human beings and society as a whole through the cultivation and enrichment of the human mind and spirit'. On its website, USC states:

> USC is a multicultural scholarly community whose diversity enriches all of our activities and interactions. As such, we aspire to create an environment in which racism, sexism, ageism, xenophobia and homophobia do not go unchallenged. The USC Code of Ethics is an integral part of our culture, and its underlying principles are tightly woven into the fabric of the USC community.

In its 2018 strategic plan, titled 'Answering the Call', USC states that its mission is to serve students, patients and communities. It claims that it must be judged not just on impact but also on integrity, and not just on endpoints but also on ethics. USC promises to engage in university-wide discussions of its current values and those new values it needs to embrace:

> We will identify ways to communicate our core values to our constituencies. We will prioritize ethical behavior as we recruit and retain university leaders. We will seek ways to identify and reward those faculty, staff, and students who exhibit and promote our core values. And we will seek ways to promote those values throughout our curricula.

Of this specific list, other universities that stood out with a strong mission statement included: KU Leuven, Duke University, University of Hong Kong, University of California Berkeley, Peking University, Stanford University, Massachusetts Institute of Technology (MIT), Cornell University, University of Zurich, Humboldt University of Berlin, Charité-Universitätsmedizin Berlin, Kyoto University and Boston University.

In addition to a purposeful mission statement, it is essential to have a strong **vision**, not just for the university but also for the community and the world. An inspirational vision begins with asking some imperative questions: What will the world look like 10 years from today due to our actions? What would we like to see? How can we contribute to realising this vision?

It is named a 'vision' for a reason. People should be able to mentally 'see' it and help others to see it. When a vision portrays a picture of a better reality, we can imagine it. Martin Luther King had a vision: 'I have a dream that my four little children will one day live in a nation where they will not be judged by the colour of their skin but by the content of their character'. This is a vision that others can share and mentally see.

As such, the vision should not be termed in verbs and actions but as a result. A vision statement describes where an organisation aspires to be upon achieving its mission. A compelling vision focuses on a positive impact, rather than on the company or university outperforming others. It inspires and engages people, such as employees, who take pride in it, know it and cite it. A vision should be others-centred, not self-centred. It is often the vision of a sustainable world and thriving community that resonates with internal and external stakeholders the most.

Of the universities we examined, only a small portion had a vision statement, and even fewer still had one that was purpose-led, inspirational and defined in terms of the envisioned result. One good example was Karolinska Institute in Sweden. It declares that its vision is 'to make a significant contribution to the improvement of human health'. This is a purpose-led vision, but it could have been phrased as an ultimate result: a world in which everyone is healthier due to the contribution of science and medicine. The vision of Queensland University in Australia is 'knowledge leadership for a better world'. It is powerful because it shows the ultimate result and connects to the university's purpose.

Values

In addition to their vision and purpose, universities often display a set of values, which are evaluative beliefs that guide our preferences and behaviour (Schwartz, 1992). Values are based on our self-concept and our ideal self: the way we would like to see ourselves and for others to see us. They can be described as desirable, trans-situational goals that vary in importance as guiding principles in people's lives.

Values define what is right and wrong and therefore are the basis of our moral approach and behaviour. According to Schwartz (1992), there are 10 universal values, which are divided by self-enhancement versus self-transcendence and by openness to change versus conservation. Self-transcended values include benevolence (preserving and enhancing the welfare of others) and universalism (caring about the welfare of all people and for nature; seeing oneself as part of a greater humanity). As such, a purpose-driven university is usually characterised by self-transcendent values, such as benevolence and universalism.

Values can set a university apart from the competition by clarifying its identity and serving as a reference point for students and staff. However, values need to be meaningful, and they only become meaningful if they mean something to people and imply action. As explained by Lencioni (2002, p. 113):

> Take a look at this list of corporate values: Communication. Respect. Integrity. Excellence. They sound pretty good, don't they? Strong, concise, meaningful. Maybe they even resemble your own company's values, the ones you spent so much time writing, debating, and revising. If so, you should be nervous. These are the corporate values of Enron, as stated in the company's 2000 annual report. And as events have shown, they're not meaningful; they're meaningless.

It is therefore critical to differentiate between *espoused values*, which are desirable by organisations, individuals and society, and *enacted values*, on which people rely to guide decisions and behaviours (Simons, 2002). Espoused values that are not enacted could be perceived as insincere and result in a loss of trust.

Clear values guide people in their attitudes and behaviour in the workplace and act as a moral compass and social glue. Therefore, value congruence in the workplace, when employees' and employers' values align, is crucial for the success of the company and the individual's wellbeing (Edwards & Cable, 2009). Clear values help to foster a long-lasting culture which, in turn, socialises newcomers and creates a sense of affiliation and pride among all employees. A purpose-driven university can attract and recruit purpose-driven students and staff to create such an alignment.

Of the top 100 universities (Times Higher Education, 2018), only 34 had their values portrayed on their website. The words *excellence* and *integrity* appeared repeatedly (as if any university would not want to be excellent). Many universities had a list of six to eight values, with no explanation of what they mean.

UC San Diego was an exceptional example. One of the top 15 research universities in the world; the university's moto is 'we make changemakers' (UC San Diego, 2019). Its vision is to 'prepare the next generation of global leaders to channel their passions into driving innovation, fuelling economic growth and making our world a better place'. UC San Diego's mission is: 'transforming California and a diverse global society by educating, by generating and disseminating knowledge and creative works, and by engaging in public service'. It was one of the few universities to clearly communicate its values, which are fully aligned with the above vision and mission:

> To be successful, UC San Diego must remain distinctive, maximize our comparative advantages, and ensure our culture and environment exemplify our values. These values, which inform and shape strategies and initiatives across the university, apply to every employee unit and campus organisation:
>
> - Collaborative and interdisciplinary activities lead to unsurpassed discoveries, technologies, cures, scholarship, and creative works that advance and enrich society.
> - Excellence in teaching, research, patient care, and a people- and service- oriented culture that supports learning, scholarly work, and public service are the norm.
> - Our focus on diversity, equity, and inclusion enables faculty, students, and staff to excel and provides an opportunity for all to succeed.
> - Our entrepreneurial spirit leads to agility, risk taking, and innovative approaches to solving problems and seizing opportunities. Public service, sustainability, integrity, and ethics are core principles guiding our activities.

Imperative Questions to Ask

Having a clear purpose, mission, vision and values, which are all intertwined and connected, is vital for obtaining a competitive advantage in our fast-changing world, engaging staff and stakeholders and attracting purpose-driven students and staff. Below are four imperative questions which could instigate an engaging conversation and help define a purpose:

(1) *Why does the world need us?* In a world of 10,000 universities, why do we need another one? Each university should be able to articulate why the world needs it in terms of the unique impact it has on people's lives, including students, academic and professional staff, the university leadership and the community.

(2) *What makes us different?* Every university wants to educate students well and lead excellent research. Every university strives to gain research funds

and boasts about its achievements. What makes our university different? It is essential to find indicators that are so unique that they could become a game-changer. Instead of providing the number of wealthy alumni and how much they make, it is valuable to share the difference that they make.

(3) *How can we transform lives?* The best way to capture purpose is to examine whom we aim to work with and what impact we have on their lives. The primary target audience could be students, but it could also be refugees, women, young girls in Afghanistan or social entrepreneurs in Africa. How can universities use their extraordinary knowledge, intellect, talent and skills to change people's lives? Moreover, in what way will universities change these people? It is a collaborative approach in which all stakeholders are partners, aiming to achieve a shared purpose.

(4) *If we were to close tomorrow, what would be lost forever?* If our university was to close tomorrow, which is unlikely, many people would need to find a new job or a new place to study. Nevertheless, what are the unique features and contributions our university has that will consequently be lost? If there is no clear answer to this question, it may be time to engage in a multi-stakeholder conversation and define our purpose.

References

Berkeley. (2019). *Berkeley strategic plan*. Retrieved from www.strategicplan.berkeley.edu/guiding-values-and-principles/

Cambridge University. (2019). *Purpose*. Retrieved from www.dictionary.cambridge.org/dictionary/english/purpose

Chandler, D. (2017). *Strategic corporate social responsibility: Sustainable value creation*. Thousand Oaks, CA: SAGE.

Christensen, C. M. (2017). *How will you measure your life?* Boston, MA: Harvard Business Review Press.

Davis, J. H., Ruhe, J. A., Lee, M., & Rajadhyaksha, U. (2007). Mission possible: Do school mission statements work? *Journal of Business Ethics, 70*(1), 99–110.

Edwards, J. R., & Cable, D. M. (2009). The value of value congruence. *Journal of Applied Psychology, 94*(3), 654–677.

EY. (2015). The business case for purpose. *Harvard Business Review*. Retrieved from www.ey.com/Publication/vwLUAssets/ey-the-business-case-for-purpose/%24FILE/ey-the-business-case-for-purpose.pdf

Gamoran, A. (2018). The future of higher education is social impact. *Stanford Social Innovation Review*. Retrieved from www.ssir.org/articles/entry/the_future_of_higher_education_is_social_impact#

Hedges, K. (2017, August 17). Five questions to help your employees find their inner purpose. *Harvard Business Review*. Retrieved from www.hbr.org/2017/08/5-questions-to-help-your-employees-find-their-inner-purpose

Hemerling, J., White, B., Swan, J., Castellana Kreisman, C., & Reed, J. B. (2018). *For corporate purpose to matter, you've got to measure it*. Boston, MA: Boston Consulting Group. Retrieved from www.bcg.com/en-au/publications/2018/corporate-purpose-to-matter-measure-it.aspx

Hollensbe, E., Wookey, C., Loughlin, H., George, G., & Nichols, V. (2014). Organizations with purpose. *Academy of Management Journal*, *57*(5), 1227–1234.

Lencioni, P. M. (2002). Make your values mean something. *Harvard Business Review*, *80*(7), 113–117.

Mackey, J., & Sisodia, R. (2014). *Conscious capitalism*. Boston, MA: Harvard Business Review Press.

MIT. (2019). *About MIT*. Retrieved from www.web.mit.edu/about/

Palmer, T. B., & Short, J. C. (2008). Mission statements in US colleges of business: An empirical examination of their content with linkages to configurations and performance. *Academy of Management Learning and Education*, *7*(4), 454–470.

Phelps, S. (2017, April 10). Understanding your why in business through the eight purpose archetypes. *Forbes*. Retrieved from www.forbes.com/sites/stanphelps/2017/04/10/understanding-your-why-in-business-through-the-eight-purpose-archetypes/#1f5d16233564

Pink, D. H. (2009). *Drive: The surprising truth about what motivates us*. New York, NY: Penguin Books.

Quinn, R. E., & Thakor, A. V. (2018). Creating a purpose-driven organization. *Harvard Business Review*, *96*(4), 78–85.

Reyes, J. R., & Kleiner, B. H. (1990). How to establish an organisational purpose. *Management Decision*, *28*(7), 51–54.

Robak, R. W., & Griffin, P. W. (2000). Purpose in life: What is its relationship to happiness, depression, and grieving? *North American Journal of Psychology*, *2*(1), 113–119.

Schwartz, S. H. (1992). Universals in the content and structure of values: Theoretical advances and empirical tests in 20 countries. *Advances in Experimental Social Psychology*, *25*(1), 1–65.

Schwartz, T., & Porath, C. (2014). The power of meeting your employees' needs. *Harvard Business Review*, *26*(6), 442–457.

Simons, T. (2002). Behavioral integrity: The perceived alignment between managers' words and deeds as a research focus. *Organization Science*, *13*(1), 18–35.

Sinek, S. (2011). *Start with why: How great leaders inspire everyone to take action*. London: Penguin Books.

Stanford University. (2019). *About Stanford*. Retrieved from www.stanford.edu/about/

Times Higher Education (THE). (2018). *World university rankings 2018*. Retrieved from www.timeshighereducation.com/world-university-rankings/2018/world-ranking#!/page/0/length/25/sort_by/rank/sort_order/asc/cols/stats

The University of Southern California (USC). (2019). *Policies and core documents*. Retrieved from www.about.usc.edu/policies/

UC San Diego. (2019). *About UC San Diego*. Retrieved from www.ucsd.edu/about/index.html

Warren, R. (2002). *The purpose driven life: What on earth am I here for?* Grand Rapids, MI: Zondervan.

Chapter 2

The Multi-level Benefits of a Strong Purpose

The Benefits of Purpose at Erasmus University, the Netherlands

> In recent years – and across the globe – we have noticed the growth of a new, conscientious generation of management students. They are focused on a variety of non-traditional career paths including sustainability, social impact and entrepreneurship. Human factors rather than just perfect test scores, huge salaries and top jobs have become increasingly important. This generation is interested in gaining an education that not only benefits themselves, but also benefits and contributes to society. In short, they want to make a positive impact on the world they live and work in. Business School and the traditional MBA have to evolve. And we acknowledge that. (Rotterdam School of Management, Erasmus University)

Erasmus University Rotterdam (EUR), named after the 15th-century humanist and theologian Desiderius Erasmus Roterodamus, is a public university located in Rotterdam, the Netherlands. EUR is currently one of the biggest universities in the Netherlands with a student population of over 29,000 and a research community of circa 1400. Scholars and students in seven faculties and two institutions work on global social challenges in the areas of health, wealth, governance and culture. The University is well known for its leading business school (Rotterdam School of Management or RSM) and has been placed in the top 100 universities in the world by major ranking bodies, including the Financial Times and Times Higher Education.

The University was founded in 1913 as the Netherlands School of Commerce through a private initiative with broad support from the Rotterdam business community. In 1937, the School was recognised, received university status and changed its name to the Netherlands School of Economics. The 1960s saw the establishment of the faculties of Law and Social Sciences, followed by Philosophy, History and Arts, and Business Administration. In 1966, the Dutch government established the Medical Faculty Rotterdam, and in 1973, the Medical Faculty Rotterdam and the Netherlands School of Economics merged, resulting in the establishment of Erasmus University Rotterdam (Erasmus University, 2019a).

The mission of Erasmus University Rotterdam is to 'understand and make progress towards solving complex societal challenges, with alignment in our core activities of education and research and in close cooperation with our partners locally and globally' (Erasmus University, 2019b). Its 2024 strategy is tagged 'Creating positive societal impact' and 'One university, one community, one goal':

> In today's rapidly changing world, society expects engagement with universities to tackle complex societal challenges together. Erasmus University Rotterdam is committed to being fully engaged with society, taking responsibility and proposing solutions for the society of the future. Our mission is: to create positive societal impact. We do it "the Erasmian way".

Erasmus University and Rotterdam School of Management use this purpose to engage students and create impact. RSM has a purpose statement of being a force for positive change and delivers its 'MBA of Value' based on an impact purpose:

> We believe in the new generation of students. A generation that is keen to solve the most complex challenges in the world. That's why we've taken a different approach to business education. We encourage our students to challenge conventions and be the change they want to see, whether it's making cities more sustainable or helping to grow local economies. We strive to give their MBA value.

This purpose attracts a large number of students to the University and its business school and creates student engagement and involvement. Students are engaged, for example, through a 'Green Office' and an Erasmus Sustainability Hub, in leading the University towards environmental sustainability. EUR students are also involved in Enactus, delivering new ventures that are aimed at benefiting the world, such as RotterJam, where lonely elderly and student volunteers jointly make delicious jam, which is then sold in stores.

The University engages its people in the journey towards purpose. Through its iWill campaign (www.rsm.nl/i-will), students and staff are encouraged to share their purpose statement. The RSM Dean shared: 'I will ensure RSM is a force for positive change in the world', connecting his personal purpose with the organisational one. 'I will give a voice to the silent', 'I will inspire people to adopt sustainable lifestyles' and 'I will create economic opportunities for my hometown' are just a few of the thousands of purpose statements collected to date. RSM shares iWill inspirational stories and present participants with the iWill awards.

To work towards its purpose statement, RSM has the 'Positive Change' initiative, to enhance the Sustainable Development Goals (or SDGs; see Chapter 3).

RSM helps to achieve the Goals through research, education and engagement and offers three videos for each SDG: by a student, an academic and a business partner. An outstanding example of SDG innovative teaching is RSM's escape room, designed to raise awareness of SDG12 (Responsible Consumption and Production). The Sustainable Food Lab offers classes on plant-based food and cooking, and most events at RSM offer vegan and vegetarian meals as a default, while meat eaters need to request the 'special meal'.

EUR benefits from high performance through cutting-edge research and teaching excellence. It has become a destination of choice for many purpose-driven students and staff. Its work on impact benefits the students and staff, the University and society at large. This is the power of a purpose-driven university to create a multi-level impact.

Introduction

Why should universities change towards purpose, define it, embed it in every aspect of their organisational life and share it with the world? Creating a purpose-driven university does not have to cost a considerable amount of money, but it does take effort and time and it is not entirely without risks. Universities should do it because purpose-driven organisations benefit people, the organisation and society (Leibson, 2018).

EY (2015), which recently defined its purpose as 'to build a better working world', published a global study in the *Harvard Business Review*: 'The business case for purpose'. Based on a global survey of 474 executives, the researchers found that 89% of executives agreed that a strong sense of collective purpose drives employee satisfaction, 80% believed it could help to increase customer loyalty, and 84% say it can affect the ability to transform. Nonetheless, although there is near unanimity in the business community about the value of purpose in driving performance, less than half of the executives surveyed said their company had articulated a strong sense of purpose and used it to make decisions and strengthen motivation. These results imply a gap between the way most people perceive the importance of having a well-defined purpose and the way they act on it, which presents an excellent opportunity to lead the way as a purpose-driven organisation and university.

However, things are changing, including in the corporate world. This year (2019), 181 Business Roundtable CEOs released and signed a new 'Statement on the Purpose of a Corporation'. All signatories committed to lead their companies for the benefit of all stakeholders and to adopt a holistic and multi-stakeholder approach to achieve this shared purpose (Business Roundtable, 2019; Ludema & Johnson, 2019). Bill McNabb, former CEO of Vanguard, declared:

> I welcome this thoughtful statement by Business Roundtable CEOs on the Purpose of a Corporation. By taking a broader, more complete view of corporate purpose, boards can focus on creating long-term value, better serving everyone – investors, employees, communities, suppliers and customers.

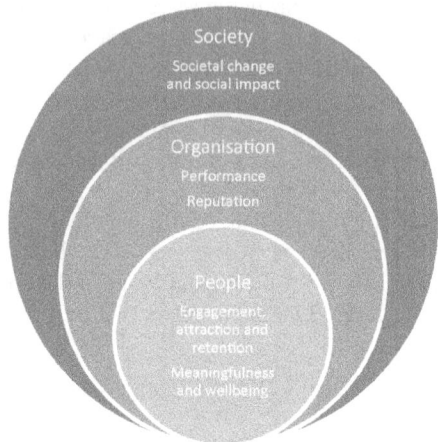

Fig. 2.1. The Multi-level Benefits of Purpose.

Indeed, research shows that purpose-driven organisations, particularly those with an impact purpose, yield remarkable benefits on the micro, meso and macro levels: for the individuals with whom the organisation works and who work for the organisation; for the organisation; and for society and the community. Fig. 2.1 summarises the benefits which will be detailed in this chapter.

This chapter will detail the benefits on each of the three levels and to the various stakeholder groups with whom universities work. Understanding the possible benefits can do more than build a strong 'business case' or a rationale to convince non-believers to make these efforts. It can also impact the way organisations develop their purpose and change towards it. For example, to yield the benefits related to employee engagement, the organisation needs to involve employees in the journey, sharing the purpose with them and making sure that stories of impact are constantly circulated so that employees gain enthusiasm for the purpose, a sense of ownership over it and a stake in the organisational purpose.

Micro-level Benefits: Changing People's Lives

While employee engagement is becoming an increasingly prominent issue for many companies and organisations, most higher education institutions do not sufficiently focus on investing in the engagement of their academic and professional staff (Deloitte Global Human Capital Trends, 2017). According to a Gallup (2017) higher education survey, 52% of faculty members were not engaged in their work, and an additional 14% were actively disengaged. Only 34% of university faculty and staff reported feeling engaged in their jobs.

Why does this matter? Because when academics do not care about their work, students are affected. Graduates were 40% more likely to be thriving in five key elements of wellbeing if they felt that a professor personally cared about them (Ellucian, 2016). University executive leaders understand this, with 80% of executives rating employee engagement as very important (Deloitte Global Human Capital Trends, 2017). Low engagement can lead to high turnover, and over 41% of survey participants said that the staff turnover in their university was very high or above average (Ellucian, 2016). As yet, not enough is done to engage people.

One effective way of increasing employee engagement and enthusiasm is through a clear purpose. In a publication titled *Employee Engagement in the Higher Education Sector*, IES (2019) asserted that a key to engagement is the individual's perception that the work undertaken is significant and has a clear purpose and meaning. Employees need to feel proud of the university for which they work and that they are making a difference. A solid connection between the individual's work and the success and impact of the organisation is essential.

A well-defined purpose gives people a clear sense of what their contribution to the organisation is and how it is part of a 'bigger picture', which brings meaning not only to their specific role but also to their work and life. As Rebecca Henderson, the John and Natty McArthur University Professor at Harvard Business School, explained:

> The sense of being part of something greater than yourself can lead to high levels of engagement, high levels of creativity, and the willingness to partner across functional and product boundaries within a company, which are hugely powerful. [...] Once they're past a certain financial threshold, many people are as motivated by intrinsic meaning and the sense that they are contributing to something worthwhile as much as they are by financial returns or status. (EY, 2015, p. 4)

Indeed, one *Harvard Business Review* study (Schwartz & Porath, 2014) showed that employees who derive meaning and significance from their work are more than three times likely to stay with their organisations – the highest single impact of any variable. These employees also reported 1.7 times higher job satisfaction and they were 1.4 times more engaged at work.

Purpose can thus lead to employee engagement and affective commitment and, consequently, to recruitment and retention of staff. A purpose-driven university can become the destination of choice for purpose-driven people who are intrinsically motivated to achieve and help the organisation achieve its goal (Deci & Ryan, 1985). To win the war for talent (Bhattacharya, Sen, & Korschun, 2008), organisations must discover a purpose that is worth committing to – one that is socially responsible, human-centred and ethical (Mercurio, 2017). Employees are searching for a value congruence with employers and are attracted to work for organisations with a clear purpose (Haski-Leventhal, Roza, & Meijs, 2017). Reid Hoffman, the executive chairman and co-founder of LinkedIn, said: 'Companies that understand the increasing emphasis of purpose in today's professional landscape improve their ability to attract such employees and also their ability to retain them for longer periods of time' (Hoffman, 2015).

Purpose is particularly critical for millennials (born between 1981 and 1996) and Generation Z (born between 1997 and 2012). According to a study done by the Society for Human Resource Management (Gurchiek, 2014), 94% of millennials want to use their skills to benefit a cause, and 57% wish that there were more company-wide service days. Attracting young employees and students is crucial for most universities, and a well-defined purpose can offer an outstanding and effective pathway.

Furthermore, when people are engaged with the purpose of the organisation they work with or study at, their physical and emotional wellbeing increase and they gain a sense of meaningfulness and happiness (Vlachos, Panagopoulos, & Rapp, 2013). As such, acting with a clear sense of purpose is part of the responsibilities of a purpose-driven university and of being a caring employer. Purpose affects the wellbeing of the individual as well as of the organisation.

When people share a compelling narrative of purpose, they develop a sense of belonging and pride (DeJaynes, 2015). Purpose can be a sturdy connector of people, connecting employees to employees, faculty to students and internal stakeholders to external ones. It can become the social glue that makes the difference between great, successful and impactful organisations and those that focus too narrowly on short-term goals and survival.

Meso-level Benefits: Helping the Organisation to Thrive

As purpose helps individuals to gain a sense of purposefulness and meaningfulness, it ultimately affects the entire organisation. An organisational impact purpose could lead to higher levels of employee and financial performance, and enhance reputation, among other benefits to the organisation. Obviously, these benefits cannot be separated from the micro-level ones, and, as such, a purpose-driven university connects and simultaneously focuses on the micro, meso and macro levels.

Due to the multiple benefits of purpose to the individual (and the consequential engagement, commitment and retention), purpose-driven organisations outperform others. Employee engagement leads to higher performance, as people are intrinsically motivated to co-achieve the organisational goal. If the organisational goal is aligned with an impact purpose for the community and for society, a spillover effect may occur, resulting in people's perception of the organisational purpose as their own, and in a joint effort to achieve it. As asserted in one *Harvard Business Review* article, 'Creating a Purpose-Driven Organisation', 'when an authentic purpose permeates the strategy and decision making, the personal good and the collective good become one'. Positive peer pressure kicks in and employees are re-energised. Collaboration increases, learning accelerates and performance climbs (Quinn & Thakor, 2018). Purpose-driven employees are motivated to give their very best at work, perform well and increase the overall collective employee performance of the company. When all employees share the same purpose and motivation, the increase in the overall performance can be substantial.

Subsequently, purpose-driven organisations can also benefit from an enhanced reputation in the community. In the age of social media, having and communicating a clear purpose can resonate with external stakeholders, including consumers, shareholders and the community. Purpose-based marketing campaigns are often shared on social media and can go viral. To illustrate, the Dove campaign, 'Real beauty sketches: You're more beautiful than you think', with the purpose of enhancing girls' and women's self-acceptance and self-esteem, had nearly 100 million combined views on YouTube. Similarly, a campaign by Western Sydney University, featuring the impact story of an alum who used to be a child soldier and is now a refugee lawyer, has gone viral in Australia and elsewhere (see Chapter 6). Some companies, such as The Body Shop, Ben & Jerry's and Patagonia are so well-known for their social purpose that their reputation is based on it. Moreover, some purpose-driven companies (e.g. Toms Shoes) hardly invest in marketing. It is time for universities to build a strong reputation in the community for being purpose-led and impactful beyond educating students and conducting research.

In addition, purpose-driven universities can attract students, and, in turn, affect their income. Here, purpose can help to resonate with students as it does for consumers in for-profit organisations because students are the university's customers and a major stakeholder group. In the Good Purpose study, Edelman (2012) found that 89% of consumers are more likely to buy from companies that have a higher purpose and support solutions to social issues. For more than half, purpose is the most important factor influencing brand choice when quality and price are equal. A university that communicates its higher purpose and acts on it could attract exceptional cohorts of students and potential leaders. This can result in consumer loyalty, which, in a university context, implies high levels of admissions, enthused students and devoted alumni.

Due to high employee engagement and performance, a positive reputation in the community and the ability to create consumer loyalty, purpose-driven organisations also do well financially. In the corporate world, this translates into shareholder value and return on investment. One study (Gartenberg, Prat, & Serafeim, 2016), which involved 500,000 people across 429 firms, suggested a positive impact on both financial performance (return on assets) and forward-looking measures of performance when the purpose is communicated with clarity. Another study (Stengel, 2018) collected data across 50,000 organisations for a decade, to also find a direct relationship between the ability of an organisation to serve a higher purpose and financial performance. This study showed that businesses with 'higher ideals' – those focusing on improving people's lives – grew three times faster than their competitors. Similarly, according to the *Purpose at Work* report (Imperative & LinkedIn, 2016), 85% of purpose-led companies had an increase in their profits, while 42% of companies with no defined purpose had a decline in revenue. Kotter and Heskett (2011) also showed that over a decade-long period, purposeful and value-driven companies outperformed their counterparts in stock price by a factor of 12.

We are yet to study how purpose-driven universities can increase their financial performance due to admission fees, generous donations, endowments and sales of patents and services, but we do have some anecdotal evidence which will be discussed in this book. For example, the former president of the University of Texas at Brownsville (see Chapter 4) managed to lead a purpose-driven fundraising campaign and achieved her financial goal due to a well-defined purpose. The goal was not only to raise funds but also to use these funds to enable students from disadvantaged backgrounds to attend college and to give hope to the local community. This purpose resonated with donors, from wealthy ones to people with just a few dollars to give.

Macro-level Benefits: Impacting Society and the Community

As the goal of this book is to increase the positive social impact that universities create in the world, it is possible to say that the macro-level benefits to society and the community are the critical ones. These are the positive changes universities can make in people's lives, beyond employing people and providing students with a degree. These benefits are the result of working with (and for) the community to do good for the world.

The macro-level benefits can be measured through outputs, short-term outcomes and long-term impacts (see Chapter 6). A university that provides educational support for local children from disadvantaged areas can measure the interactions between these children and the academic staff who volunteer to help them (activities), the improvement in the school results for that year (outputs) or the long-term changes in participants' employability, self-esteem and quality of life (outcomes), and community wellbeing and resilience, employment and poverty (impact). All of these could be the macro-level benefits of a purpose-driven university.

To illustrate, Drexel University in Philadelphia works to bring West Philadelphia (which it calls 'The Promise Zone') out of poverty through its civic engagement (Drexel University, 2019). While it cites a definition of civic engagement ('individual and collective actions designed to identify and address issues of public concern'), it also says that, at Drexel, it boils down to being a part of the community:

> As an anchor institution we have made a commitment to the Philadelphia community we are part of. We are a private institution working for public good, and much of our work is in creative collaboration with our campus neighbors. We carry out this mission through our academic and research functions, through our business operations, and through the volunteer power of our students and employees.

Drexel University's Office of University and Community Partnerships works through neighbourhood partnerships, civic engagement, education and economic development to address issues of poverty, housing affordability, health, public safety and legal aid to support and strengthen the local community. Its three dimensions of civic engagement are service and volunteering; institutional investment (e.g. social procurement and employment); and academic integration. Drexel's interventions start from an early age (0–3, with early childcare) through schools (mentoring and educational support) to young adults and their career.

As a result, Drexel University was able to create a positive impact in the local community and beyond. Its economic impacts include a US$30 million rise in salaries paid to West Philadelphia residents in 2018, and another nearly US$10 million invested in the neighbourhood. As for education, in 2018 Drexel reached over 4000 residents and distributed 15,000 free books to West Philadelphia families. The University served nearly 7000 young people and provided 3500 backpacks with school supplies to local children (Drexel University, 2018).

While the University is yet to measure the long-term impact on society, the indicators above show many macro-level benefits. The focus on societal impact can also benefit employees, students and the organisation. For example, 75% of incoming first-year students indicated that Drexel's commitment to civic engagement was an essential part of their decision to choose Drexel, demonstrating that, through purpose, Drexel became the destination of choice for purpose-driven students. Furthermore, 87% of students believed that they could make a positive change in their community, showing that leading by example can be inspiring, engaging and create a momentum of impact.

Universities have an enormous potential to benefit the communities in which they operate, the global community and the environment. It takes a focused effort to become a force for good and to achieve these benefits. While benefiting society can create a social return on investment, it can also create a positive impact on the university if the aim is to benefit society first.

Imperative Questions to Ask

(1) *Who might benefit from our work towards an impact purpose?* Identifying all the stakeholders who could benefit from the impact purpose on a multi-level analysis (namely, micro, meso, and macro levels) is essential, even in early stages. By recognising the people, organisations and communities who would benefit, the university embarks on a stakeholder mapping which can serve it in creating alliances towards purpose. If the aim is to maximise impact for as many stakeholders as possible, such an analysis is crucial.

(2) *Which level of benefits (micro, meso or macro) should be prioritised?* While I asserted here that the macro-level to society and the community should be prioritised, this is not always the case. In some universities, employee engagement is so low that the university needs to focus on them in early stages, involve them in the impact purpose and create a sense of meaningfulness through community outreach. However, if universities only use the idea of purpose to benefit themselves, the process will not yield the same results as genuinely and holistically involvement in the community.

Becoming a purpose-driven university for short-term wins will always imply doing less.

(3) *How do we measure the impact and benefits?* For organisations to yield the benefits of purpose, they need to measure it (Hemerling, White, Swan, Castellana Kreisman, & Reed, 2018). This implies measuring the purpose the university aims to create as well as the benefits it yields for micro-level, meso-level and macro-level actors. While there will be an overlap between the two, many organisations, including large multinational with a strong CSR, only measure the impact it intended to create and not the additional or unintended benefits. As such, a university that uses its power to improve children's education in disadvantaged neighbourhoods might only measure its impact on the children, but not on the university's staff and students, or the children's families and communities. For more information on measuring impact and benefits, see Chapter 6.

References

Bhattacharya, C. B., Sen, S., & Korschun, D. (2008). Using corporate social responsibility to win the war for talent. *MIT Sloan Management Review*, *49*(2), 35–46.

Business Roundtable. (2019). *Our commitment*. Retrieved from www.opportunity.businessroundtable.org/ourcommitment

Deci, E. L., & Ryan, R. M. (1985). The general causality orientations scale: Self-determination in personality. *Journal of Research in Personality*, *19*(2), 109–134.

DeJaynes, T. (2015). "Where I'm from" and belonging: A multimodal, cosmopolitan perspective on arts and inquiry. *E-Learning and Digital Media*, *12*(2), 183–198.

Deloitte Global Human Capital Trends. (2017). *Rewriting the rules for the digital age*. Retrieved from www.www2.deloitte.com/content/dam/Deloitte/us/Documents/human-capital/hc-2017-global-human-capital-trends-us.pdf

Drexel University. (2018). *Office of university and community partnership: Dashboard 2017–2018*. Philadelphia, PA: Drexel University.

Drexel University. (2019). *Civic engagement at Drexel*. Retrieved from www.drexel.edu/civicengagement

Edelman. (2012). *The good purpose study*. Retrieved from www.slideshare.net/EdelmanJapan/2012-edelman-goodpurpose

Ellucian. (2016). *Retention and student success: Implementing strategies that make a difference*. Retrieved from www.ellucian.com/assets/en/white-paper/whitepaper-retention-and-student-success.pdf

Erasmus University. (2019a). *History*. Retrieved from www.eur.nl/en/about-eur/organisation-administration/tradition-and-history/history

Erasmus University. (2019b). *Strategy and policy*. Retrieved from www.eur.nl/en/about-eur/strategy-and-policy

EY. (2015). *The business case for purpose*. Retrieved from www.ey.com/Publication/vwLUAssets/ey-the-business-case-for-purpose/%24FILE/ey-the-business-case-for-purpose.pdf

Gallup. (2017). *The engaged university*. Retrieved from www.gallup.com/education/194321/higher-education-employee-engagement.aspx

Gartenberg, C., Prat, A., & Serafeim, G. (2016, September). *Corporate purpose and financial performance*. Working Paper No. 17-023. Harvard Business School, MA.

Gurchiek, K. (2014). *Millennials' desire to do good defines workplace culture*. Retrieved from www.shrm.org/ResourcesAndTools/hr-topics/behavioral-competencies/global-and-cultural-effectiveness/Pages/Millennial-Impact.aspx

Haski-Leventhal, D., Roza, L., & Meijs, L. C. (2017). Congruence in corporate social responsibility: Connecting the identity and behavior of employers and employees. *Journal of Business Ethics, 143*(1), 35–51.

Hemerling, J., White, B., Swan, J., Castellana Kreisman, C., & Reed, J. B. (2018). *For corporate purpose to matter, you've got to measure it*. Boston, MA: Boston Consulting Group. Retrieved from www.bcg.com/en-au/publications/2018/corporate-purpose-to-matter-measure-it.aspx

Hoffman, R. (2015). *The power of purpose at work*. Retrieved from www.linkedin.com/pulse/power-purpose-work-reid-hoffman/

Imperative & LinkedIn. (2016). *Purpose at work: 2016 global report*. Retrieved from www.business.linkedin.com/content/dam/me/business/en-us/talent-solutions/resources/pdfs/purpose-at-work-global-report.pdf

Institute for Employment Studies (IES). (2019). *Employee engagement in the higher education sector*. Retrieved from www.blogs.shu.ac.uk/hallamleaders/files/2018/01/employee_engagement_in_the_he_sector_-_evidence_review.pdf

Kotter, J. P., & Heskett, J. L. (2011). *Corporate culture and performance*. New York, NY: Free Press.

Leibson, H. (2018). The power of purpose driven. *Forbes*. Retrieved from www.forbes.com/sites/hayleyleibson/2018/01/25/the-power-of-purpose-driven/#6b1998285dca

Ludema, J., & Johnson, M. (2019). *The purpose of the corporation? Business roundtable advances the conversation, now we all need to contribute*. Retrieved from www.forbes.com/sites/amberjohnson-jimludema/2019/08/20/the-purpose-of-the-corporation/#66b87e803846

Mercurio, Z. (2017). *Think millennials are purpose-driven? Meet generation Z*. Retrieved from www.huffingtonpost.com/entry/think-millennials-are-purpose-driven-meet-generation_us_5a1da9f3e4b04f26e4ba9499

Quinn, R. E., & Thakor, A. V. (2018). Creating a purpose-driven organization. *Harvard Business Review, 96*(4), 78–85.

Schwartz, T., & Porath, C. (2014). The power of meeting your employees' needs. *Harvard Business Review, 26*(6), 442–457.

Stengel, J. (2018). *Why purpose?* Retrieved from www.jimstengel.com/purpose

Vlachos, P. A., Panagopoulos, N. G., & Rapp, A. A. (2013). Feeling good by doing good: Employee CSR-induced attributions, job satisfaction, and the role of charismatic leadership. *Journal of Business Ethics, 118*(3), 577–588.

Chapter 3

Responsibility, Ethics and Sustainability in Higher Education Institutions: A Holistic Approach

Simon Fraser University: Leading Sustainability in a Whole-of-the-Community Engaging Way

Simon Fraser University (SFU) is a public research university in British Columbia, Canada. With a humble beginning in 1965 with only 2500 students, SFU has grown to more than 30,000 students and 6500 faculty and staff. Its vision is to be Canada's most community-engaged research university (Simon Fraser University, 2019a):

> An engaged university: To be the leading engaged university defined by its dynamic integration of innovative education, cutting-edge research, and far-reaching community engagement.

SFU focuses on societal needs through its research. In addition, SFU's strategic vision portrays its commitment to sustainability:

> SFU will pursue ecological, social and economic sustainability through its programs and operations. Through teaching and learning, research and community engagement, SFU will seek and share solutions. In its own operations, it will develop and model best practices, from minimizing its ecological footprint, to maximizing its social health and economic strength.

To achieve these important goals, in 2016, SFU invited its entire community to envision the University's sustainable future. Over 4000 stakeholders, including students, staff and the University leadership, worked together in an innovative engagement process to create SFU's 20-year sustainability vision and goals. SFU takes a holistic approach which has led to many initiatives across campus, including a zero-waste project (to date, 70% of its waste has been diverted from landfill). SFU has over 30 certified sustainable buildings, and over 250 undergraduate courses and 119 postgraduate courses which include elements of sustainability. Almost all students (91%) use a sustainable commute to get to campus, as do 73% of employees. Impressively, SFU has invested CA$4.5 million in sustainability investment funds and $11.5 million into socially responsible mutual funds (Simon Fraser University, 2019a, 2019b).

But it is not just environmental sustainability that is at the heart of SFU; it is also social responsibility. In 2017, SFU became an Ashoka U Changemaker Campus 'to support and inspire the next generation of change-makers, and to help them find ways to build a better society'. Ashoka U is the world's largest network of social entrepreneurs, and change-makers and its 40 member institutions are committed to working together to transform higher education and advance change-making across all sectors. Some inspirational examples include: The Passport to Leadership (helping students to develop foundational skills for change-making); Canada's first Master of Education in Arts for Social Change; and 'SFU Innovates', a university-wide innovation and social innovation strategy, dedicated to mobilising knowledge and developing leaders with the objective of building a stronger, healthier and more sustainable society.

Introduction

As universities need a clear impact purpose to engage all stakeholders and create a long-lasting impact in the world, it is valuable to utilise existing concepts and frameworks to achieve these goals. While this book is focused on the purpose-driven university, its underlying approach is based on the ideas of sustainability and social responsibility.

Universities can learn from other sectors of the economy in terms of their approach to sustainability and social responsibility. In the last few decades, there has been an enormous shift in business and governmental operations, with an emphasis on sustainable development and the United Nations Sustainable Development Goals (SDGs). There is remarkable work being done in social innovation and in using the power of business to address society's major issues, some of which can be implemented in the context of higher education.

As such, this chapter will leverage existing frameworks and examples using social responsibility, consciousness, sustainability and the SDGs to inspire universities in finding their purpose through their actions. This will be followed by a holistic approach to the purpose-driven university.

Socially Responsible Universities

Social responsibility is mostly used in the context of corporations (i.e. corporate social responsibility or CSR). According to Matten and Moon (2008), at the core of CSR is the idea that it reflects the social imperatives and the social consequences of business success. These authors defined social responsibility as a 'role within the wider formal and informal institutions for society's interests and concerns' (p. 409), including the values, norms and rules that result in addressing stakeholder issues. In addition, a more holistic approach is found in the definition of strategic CSR. Strategic CSR is about aligning what the organisation does as part of its social responsibility with what the organisation stands for, and with its strategy and core operations (Haski-Leventhal, 2018). Werther and Chandler (2011, p. 40) defined strategic CSR as:

> The incorporation of a holistic CSR perspective within a firm's strategic planning and core operations so that the firm is managed in the interest of a broad set of stakeholders to achieve maximum economic and social value over the medium to long term.

The strategic approach could be implemented in universities. As explained in Chapter 1, it is essential to define the differentiating point and unique value proposition of the university, beyond educating students and striving for excellent research, as these are what every single university in the world does. The unique value proposition may be based on the university's history (such as the founders' stories and goals, or crucial events in its past), its location (serving specific communities and groups) or the type of students it attracts (with a focus on excellence or inclusion). However, the most engaging value proposition can be revealed in terms of the unique impact purpose a university has and its contribution to society.

As part of CSR, organisations usually examine their environmental, social and governance (ESG) duties. Recently, a growing number of college endowments in the USA explored more holistic approaches to sustainable investing. Several American university endowment funds were among the first institutional investors to strive for ESG in investing. According to a survey with higher education institutions, including Harvard University, the University of Michigan and Northwestern University, these universities held $317 billion in ESG assets at the start of 2018, 8.2% higher than in 2016 (Harty & Stone, 2018).

Furthermore, many universities are engaged in community-giving of time and money (or philanthropy), through their students, employees and alumni. For example, many universities offer their students opportunities to volunteer either via service learning (courses combining volunteering, reflection and learning) or through other opportunities on or out of campus. The idea of employees volunteering has entered many higher education institutions, and academic and professional staff are often encouraged to volunteer, while some universities go further in organising the volunteer opportunities and offering paid leave to volunteer. Many universities are not only on the receiving side of donations but can also use their financial resources to donate and match the donations of their employees to charities.

However, this giving is often based on 'random acts of charity'. The charities and targets are often selected randomly or according to personal preferences. Being strategic about social responsibility implies that universities align their commitments to society and the community with their strategic vision and what they stand for. Instead of giving money to various charities, it would be more strategic for a university to help with education – of school children, students in the developing world or their own students. Such endeavours are better aligned with what a university stands for. In the same vein, employee volunteering can use people's talent and skills to help others more effectively. What universities are never short of is talented people.

Nevertheless, holistic social responsibility is more than philanthropy and giving back to the community. Responsible organisations, including universities, examine how they generate revenue, not just how they distribute some of it in the community. Strategic social responsibility is holistic, and it includes every aspect of the organisation's conduct, from people management (including outsourcing), through the content of the curriculum, to the impact education creates in the world. Examining the entire value chain and impact more holistically, working with all stakeholders to integrate them into the organisation and its work and adopting a broad view of the university's responsibilities are the first steps in achieving strategic social responsibility.

One example of how broad social responsibility can be in higher education is gender equity. Men still hold more than three-quarters of full professorships in the USA (with similar percentages in many other countries in the Western world, and even higher numbers in others). The number of female professors is especially low in STEM faculties (Viefers, Christie, & Ferdos, 2006). Women's share of full professorships has increased only marginally over the past few decades. A 2006 report showed that female associate professors were less likely to be promoted than their male counterparts, and that it took women up to three and a half years longer than men to advance to full professorships, with women at doctoral universities lagging farthest behind (Misra, Lundquist, Holmes, & Agiomavritis, 2011). Socially responsible universities have an anti-discrimination policy, a gender equity strategy and innovative ways to avoid unconscious bias. For example, some universities have now moved to a 'blind review' of applications, where first names and gender are removed. Others advertise for jobs with a clear call for women to apply, while offering working conditions that are attractive to women (Winchester & Browning, 2015).

Ethics in Higher Education

Responsible universities are based on the foundation of a moral approach, ethical behaviour, transparency and accountability. Unfortunately, universities have had their fair share of unethical behaviour and scandals. In 2019, the university admissions scandal in the USA attracted abundant attention from the media and the public. More than 50 wealthy Americans, including some celebrities, were arrested for bribing top universities' officials to get students admitted. This scandal ignited a discussion on equal opportunities in the USA and how wealthy people get an unfair advantage in the American system. In the past, some universities were involved in corruption, unethical behaviour of their senior leadership, sexual harassment and abuse. The unethical behaviour of some students, explicitly or implicitly tolerated or even encouraged by the university, also led to some negative headlines.

However, ethical issues in higher education institutions are important beyond the unethical behaviour of individuals or departments. Ethical issues include, for example, the moral stand of a university on free speech and other freedoms on campus, and the right balance between academic freedom and setting boundaries to hate speech. It is about equipping students (and others) with the ability to engage in moral discussions respectfully and to understand the difference between ethical debates that are morally acceptable (e.g. abortion rights) and those that are not (e.g. whether Jews and Black people should be allowed on campus). Interestingly, searching for the words 'universities' and 'ethics' (and their synonyms) mostly yields results on teaching ethics courses in higher education institutions, particularly in business and medical schools, and discussion on the ethical behaviour of universities is not prominent enough.

As such, universities must align their actions with purpose and values to demonstrate ethical behaviour. Universities need to ask: what are we doing, in our teachings and actions, to encourage students to be responsible and ethical, and are we doing enough to lead by example? This is the litmus test for a responsible and ethical university.

Ethics in higher education transcends teaching ethics or even proclaiming the values of integrity and honesty. Ethical values can have implications for every action the university takes. Amy Gutmann, a professor and the current president of the University of Pennsylvania (whose story will be told in the next chapter), gave an inspirational speech on ethics in higher education in 1991, which is available on YouTube.[1] Gutmann said:

> Fine. There is a place for ethics in higher education. But then, let me ask each and every one of you some follow up questions [...]: Whose ethics or what ethics should professors teach in the classroom? [...] What ethics should guide universities' fundraisers dealing with donors? Should they accept money tied to purposes that the university would not otherwise want to pursue? What ethics should guide admitting officers in deciding whom to admit? [...] What ethics should guide administrators in enforcing rules of conduct? [...] What ethics should guide universities' presidents in making policy and setting the moral tone of the university? Should they seek out a financial partnership with the government? Should they permit faculty to claim academic freedom?

These are imperative ethical questions that should initiate a discourse, policy and proactive behaviour in every university, instead of only responding to ad hoc situations presenting complex ethical dilemmas and circumstances. Universities need to take an ethical position that aligns with their mission and values because not taking a stand is taking an ethical stand. As Gutmann illustrated: by not

---

[1] www.youtube.com/watch?v=tqt8BM3aJmQ.

teaching ethics, we teach students ethics because we teach them that ethics have no value in our institution (and, perhaps, in their future leadership) and that rules and policy need no moral defence. Universities cannot be 'ethically neutral', regardless of their actions and policies. 'Even if you are not interested in ethics, ethics is still interested in you', claimed Gutmann.

Conscious Universities

A few years ago, John Mackey, the then CEO of Wholefood Markets, and Professor Raj Sisodia, wrote a book that could change the way we look at our economy, businesses and work. *Conscious Capitalism* (Mackey & Sisodia, 2014) asserted that capitalism is not inheritably bad, but that some related ideas, such as maximising profits at any cost, led to it creating a negative impact on society and the world. Conscious capitalism takes the best of this system and offers a significant change in economic thought and the role of business in society.

A conscious organisation works according to four main principles (or tenets): higher purpose and core values; stakeholder integration; conscious leadership; and conscious culture and management. The *higher purpose* was discussed in the previous chapter, explaining that it is based on the reason we exist and our contribution to the world. *Stakeholder integration* will be further discussed in Chapter 4, but, in a nutshell, it is the way all stakeholders (including staff, students, alumni, suppliers, donors and the community) are connected to the purpose and integrated into the university. Stakeholder integration suggests shifting away from a 'zero-sum game', in which one stakeholder wins when another loses, to a win-win-win situation because all stakeholders share the same purpose. Conscious organisations are led by *conscious leaders*, who have a high emotional and spiritual intelligence. They are motivated by service both to the purpose and to stakeholders, not by the pursuit of power or personal enrichment. Such leaders, as will be further discussed in Chapter 4, develop, inspire, mentor and engage while leading by example. Finally, a conscious organisation is known for its *conscious cultures*, driven by and based on the foundation that is its purpose. A conscious culture provides everyone in the organisation with a deep sense of meaning. It does so by cultivating trust, accountability, caring, transparency, integrity, loyalty and egalitarianism (Mackey & Sisodia, 2014). By adopting these four tenets, but mostly by becoming a university with a higher purpose, higher education institutions can help raise the consciousness of students, staff, leaders and others, which can then assist them in creating a positive impact and achieving their purpose.

Sustainable Universities

The concept of a sustainable university is usually associated with being 'green' or environmentally friendly: recycling, waste management and renewable energy. Some universities may adopt a long-term approach to sustainability and aim to reduce their carbon footprint or become carbon-neutral in the next few years.

Sustainability, however, is broader than practices, which may have a limited impact on the environment. A sustainable university is about adopting a long-term approach and a perception that sees humans as part of a greater ecosystem. It aims to work within this ecosystem to ensure the survival of this planet and all species living on it.

Sustainability was defined by the Brundtland report (1987) in these broader terms and based on the necessity not only to change people's and organisations' actions but also their mindset. Sustainability is 'meeting the needs of the present without compromising the ability of future generations to meet their own needs' (Brundtland, 1987, p. 16). This is a thought-provoking definition as it does not refer to the 'wants' of the current generation, which are beyond the capacity of this planet, but to meeting the 'needs' of everyone (including all those in developing countries).

This definition and its related approach should resonate with universities, given their work with future generations. There is enormous potential for higher education institutions to use their power, resources and knowledge to meet the needs of present and future generations everywhere, and thus define their purpose.

According to Hart et al. (2016), at one level academia has already risen to the sustainability challenge, through the new field of sustainability science, but the traditional academy lacks an effective institutional structure and culture for accelerating progress towards sustainability. Indeed, an increasing number of universities are implementing environmental solutions within their campus. These include solar energy installations, energy use and greenhouse gas commitments, and introducing sustainability into the teaching curriculum. However, there is still considerable progress to be made.

Higher education institutions can become more environmentally friendly by adopting long-term thinking, using their endowments and investments in ecological companies and shifting to sustainable procurement. The billions of dollars spent on purchasing products that are used on campus, from toilet paper to vehicles, can be directed to increase the positive impact of engagement in society. Many universities are built on large areas of fruitful soil which can be turned into community gardens and produce fresh fruit and vegetables, while also cultivating bees and other pollinators.

Many stakeholders now realise the significance of contributing to a sustainable future and mitigating climate change. If a university is not sustainable, its stakeholders may hold it accountable. For example, students have started monitoring higher education institutions and their actions regarding their environment, initiating their own sustainability ranking. While Cambridge University is ranked as one of the top universities in the world in terms of education and research, students ranked it only 67th in the UK based on its sustainability efforts (People and Planet, 2019).

There are outstanding examples of universities and colleges changing their values and actions to become more sustainable. The University of Copenhagen has the 'Green Lighthouse' building, which generates its own energy from solar cells and panels, storing excess energy underground. The Green Mountain

College in Vermont generates energy for its campus by burning cow manure. The University of Canterbury, New Zealand, has on-site community gardens where students can grow their own organic produce, while Canada's University of Northern British Columbia offers on-campus markets with local produce. The University of Lausanne, Switzerland, disposes of organic waste by sending it to a nearby farm, which uses it to produce organic fertilisers and biogas fuel. Some universities, such as the University of Oslo, Norway, encourage their students and staff to use green transportation (electric cars, trains and bicycles) through a variety of incentives and enablers.

The Sustainable Development Goals

An essential component of a sustainable university is sustainable development and the sustainable development goals (SDGs), which can help guide universities as a compass for the future. The SDGs are 17 global goals with 169 targets, which were adopted by all heads of state in 2015 to be achieved by 2030 (see Fig. 3.1). They represent an inter-governmental agreement among the member states of the United Nations to promote global sustainable development based on universal principles of international cooperation. The goals include matters that are crucial for humanity and the planet, from ending poverty and hunger to gender equality and sustainable cities (United Nations, 2019). The fourth goal, quality education, is particularly important for higher education institutions: 'to ensure inclusive and equitable quality education and promote lifelong learning opportunities for all'.

Fig. 3.1. The United Nations Sustainable Development Goals.
Source: United Nations (2019).

While these global goals were committed to by governments, they also create an enormous obligation and opportunity for the private and community sectors. Many corporate organisations, not-for-profit organisations, local governments, social enterprises and even individuals are taking action to help the world achieve the SDGs by 2030. Subsequently, universities can play a major role in introducing the SDGs to their students and, more importantly, helping to achieve and measure them through research, education and other activities (Levi & Rothstein, 2018). When it comes to the SDGs, universities have a teaching role, a collaborative role, an evidence-based knowledge role, a measuring role and an advocating role to play (Hovmöller, 2019).

In addition to SDG4 (quality education), other SDGs also present a great challenge and an opportunity for universities worldwide. Equipping students with the awareness and capabilities to address issues such as poverty and hunger can help them become business and social leaders who help achieve these goals. Stanford University, which was mentioned in Chapter 1, does so with its Center on Poverty and Inequality (SDG1). Erasmus University (Chapter 2) creates a whole-organisation commitment to the SDGs while working in partnership with external stakeholders to further enhance issues such as responsible consumption and production (SDG12).

The SDGs are already transforming the way universities operate. In Japan, Hokkaido University's Graduate School of Infectious Diseases is using SDG3 – the goal on good health and wellbeing – to guide its research. In Ghana, meanwhile, All Nations University College's work on empowering women through education is based on SDG5 on gender equality (Straub, 2019).

The Sustainable Development Solutions Network (SDSN) is an excellent source of information and tools for universities who want to focus on the SDGs. It has published a guide for higher education (SDSN, 2017), which outlines the prominence of the SDGs for universities and details the steps they can take to help lead the sustainable development movement. The guide explains that the SDGs can help universities by creating an increased demand for SDG-related education; providing a comprehensive and globally accepted definition of a responsible university; and offering a framework for demonstrating impact. On the other hand, universities can help with the SDGs by doing the following:

- Provide knowledge, innovations and solutions to the SDGs.
- Create current and future SDG implementers.
- Demonstrate how to support, adopt and implement SDGs in governance, operations and culture.
- Develop cross-sectoral leadership to guide the SDG response.

The guide then details how universities' internal and external actions can contribute to the SDGs, from paying employees and suppliers fairly to researching climate change. It suggests taking a whole-of-university approach to deepen their engagement with the SDGs, starting with mapping what the university is already doing in this space, building internal capacity and ownership, prioritising, integrating and monitoring.

> **Box 3.1. Steps towards the SDGs**
>
> Weybrecht (2017) suggested that universities take several steps towards the SDGs, including:
>
> - Ensure everyone on campus knows what the goals are and why they are important.
> - Identify which SDGs are material to the university.
> - Embed the SDGs into the curriculum, assignments and class discussions.
> - Explore innovative solutions.
> - Facilitate interdisciplinary and multi-stakeholder discussions to move the goals forward.
> - Use the SDGs to guide research priorities and impact.
> - Develop partnerships to advance the goals.
> - Report on these efforts and impact in relation to the SDGs.

Monash University in Australia is addressing the SDGs by motivating students through an online engagement platform named 'Take One Step'. Students use the platform to learn about related issues, commit to an SDG-inspired change in their own life (e.g. reducing food waste) and document their progress. The vision is to turn Take One Step into an international collaboration platform for students across the globe.

As of 2019, *Times Higher Education* (THE, 2019) publishes a global university ranking using the institutions' success in delivering the SDGs. Ranking 462 universities from 76 nations, New Zealand's University of Auckland, which is ranked 200–250 in the regular THE global ranking, came first in impact ranking (see Chapter 7). Another university on the top 10 list is the Swedish University of Gothenburg (2019), which aims to contribute to solutions of regional and global problems:

> Our programme catalogue is very broad, reflecting not only the needs of students and the surrounding world but also our responsibility for lifelong learning and promoting the general level of knowledge in society. We are engaged in close cooperation with the surrounding society, work for sustainable development and are an active and appreciated provider of knowledge.

Gothenburg School of Business, Economics and Law published a document titled 'Our Fundamental Values', in which it commits to equal value and treatment of all people; democracy, freedom of speech and other fundamental human rights; and the achievement of the SDGs. The School introduced 'Sustainability Days' – three full days focusing on sustainability and the SDGs from various perspectives. The SDGs are currently included in all of their postgraduate programmes; however, the school declares: 'how to best integrate the 17 SDGs and not create "silos" is one of our challenges for the future since one of the aims of Agenda 2030 is to recognise the interlinkages between different sectors, actors and goals'.

The Holistic Approach to a Purpose-Driven University

Based on the above concepts and approaches (namely strategic CSR, ethics, sustainability and the SDGs), it becomes clear that for a university to become purpose-driven, it needs to adopt a holistic approach and align its purpose with its impact in every aspect of its existence. Academic institutions offer a combination of teaching, research and service, while some focus mainly on one part of the academic triangle and others on all three. The division between these three foci often defines the university, its actions and possibly its mission. It can affect its decision-making, fundraising strategies, leadership, allocation of time and effort and even promotion criteria. A purpose-driven university needs to ensure that each part of the academic triangle is aligned with the purpose.

Boyer's (1990) Model of Scholarship revolutionised higher education, as it offered a more holistic and connected approach to the three aspects of higher education and the meaning of being a scholar. Instead of focusing mainly on research, Boyer spoke about four aspects of scholarship:

(1) The scholarship of *discovery*: original research that advances knowledge and creates an impact.
(2) The scholarship of *integration*: synthesis of information across disciplines, topics and time. This is also the integration between research (discovery) and teaching, such as through research-led teaching or teaching-focused research.
(3) The scholarship *of teaching and learning:* this is at the core of higher education institutions and Boyer speaks of teachers who are knowledgeable, informed, creative and inspired.
(4) The scholarship of *application* (or engagement): serving people and institutions within and outside the university, including in the community, and creating an impact. This can mean applying one's research and teaching to make a difference in the industry, in the community and to policy. The scholarship of engagement cuts across the categories of academic scholarship and incorporates reciprocal practices of civic engagement. Through teaching and discovery, scholars communicate and work with communities to address public issues (Anigma, 2016).

Each of these aspects of scholarship can be harnessed as part of the transformation to a purpose-driven university. Research can be more impactful by focusing on enhancing people's quality of life and community wellbeing. Teaching can be more purpose-driven to focus on the impact on students and the contribution they later make to society. Service and engagement can be better aligned with community outreach and making a difference. The transformation in the way we assess research, teaching and service can then alter the basis of academic promotion. These four aspects – impactful research; purpose-driven teaching; genuine service, engagement and citizenship; and impact-based promotion – will be discussed next.

Impactful Research

Scientific research has the power to change people and transform our society. Medical research saves lives, and environmental research can save our planet. Research in business management can transform organisations and industry and shape our economy, while research in psychology impacts people's wellbeing. Research in all disciplines can change our intuitive truths and shift paradigms, impact practices, policy and further research.

Ashwin (2015) argued that since the turn of the millennium, there has been an increasing expectation for research to benefit society. It is very reasonable to expect research to lead to wider social benefits. Individual research projects contribute to collective bodies of knowledge in a discipline or professional field. It is these bodies of knowledge that lead to impact, not individual studies.

Yet, with all this remarkable impact, many universities measure research impact by the number of outputs (i.e. academic articles), level of research outlets (preferably top-tier journals) and citation number. Universities use bibliometric indicators, including journals' impact factor, citation rates and H-Indices, as the primary measures of academic excellence. Research quality measurement exercises, such as Excellence in Research for Australia (ERA), are problematic and limited because of quantitative bibliometrics that measure and define research output as the number of academic publications and not as the longer-term benefits that research might bring to health, society or the economy (Smith, Crookes, & Crookes, 2013).

Many academic scholars mention the number of books and articles they have published but do not explain how their research changed people's lives. Higher education institutions focus on research input and output, instead of on outcomes and macro-level impact. Changing this would substantially alter the way academics write their academic curriculum vitae.

There are alternatives. Some scholars (e.g. Milat, Bauman, & Redman, 2015) suggest that academics should provide a 'narrative of impact', 'impact statements' or 'impact narratives', instead of just quantitative data on their research impact, and share stories of change. There are global efforts to develop systems which include this type of impact assessment. Such initiatives include: 'Research' by RAND corporation in Europe; Program Assessment Rating Tool (PART) in the USA; Evaluating Research in Context (ERiC) in the Netherlands; and the Research Quality Framework (RQF) in Australia. They all argue for the measurement and evaluation of research impact using non-bibliometric, quantitative methods. Some universities, such as the University of Wollongong in Australia, map research output according to the SDGs.

Being even more courageous, some scholars discuss their unintended negative research impact. This is significant because awareness of a possible negative research impact can bring attention and remedy to such issues. Possible negative impacts are precisely why a high number of universities have an ethical approval process for new studies. Nonetheless, even studies that receive ethical approval and are based on the best of intentions can have a negative impact. While I was working on this chapter, Professor Andrew Crane from the University of Bath in the UK, who conducted an international study on modern slavery, shared his thoughts on this topic in his blog (Crane, 2019):

> 'If you put these things in your report it will kill our industry'. The words [...] stop me dead in my tracks. [...] Obviously, we have no intention of harming the industry, but hearing these concerns reiterated to us how careful we need to be about what kind of impact we might create [through our research] and how and to whom we should communicate our findings. What would happen if critics in the media, or NGOs, took our research and used it to push for changes that we did not want to see happen? And how exactly should we highlight problems in the industry in ways that would not harm our informants? [We need] to carefully evaluate the potential outcomes of different courses of action in order to assess which pathways to impact might deliver the most overall benefit, even if that could mean some stakeholders being disadvantaged. [...] Academics can't control all the impacts that derive from their research, but they can be better prepared and supported in recognising where the wrong kinds of impact can emerge and what safeguards need to be put in place to minimise their effects.

This is an example of outstanding reflective practice, which more academics and researchers need to be encouraged to undertake. Purpose-driven universities need to measure the full impact of the research done by their staff, including the positive and negative impacts, intended and unintended, to assess how research assists in meeting their purpose.

Purpose-Driven Teaching

What is the purpose of teaching? If we go back to the Golden Circle (Sinek, 2011), most universities and faculty know *what* they teach and *how* they teach it. Every university in the world details its faculties, departments, degrees and units. They might even share how they teach it – face to face or online, through traditional or experiential learning, in small or large classes. They often boast about *who* teaches, or the high academic level of the faculty teaching these courses. However, very few universities in the world share *why* they teach – what their teaching philosophy is and how their teaching is aligned with their overall purpose statement.

Here is a fascinating demonstration of the above. Cornell University, an Ivy League research university in New York, proposes that its academic staff who apply for promotion should discuss their teaching philosophy by including:

- their conception of teaching and learning;
- a description of how they teach;
- justification for why they teach that way.

These guidelines are not about teaching purpose or philosophy, but a justification of content. Similar to the previous discussion on research impact, teaching impact is often conveyed through students' evaluations and results. At the university level, teaching quality is usually measured by the number of people who graduated, retention rates and perhaps graduates' success in terms of employment and income. These are all important, but none measure the impact of teaching.

Academic research on the impact of higher education regularly focuses on immediate results, such as employability or entrepreneurial intentions, or on outcomes such as student satisfaction and even commitment to donate. Universities have been measuring teaching outcomes for centuries, through assessments, marks and teaching evaluations. However, the time is ripe to include new indicators of teaching impact. Universities could examine long-term outputs such as (global) citizenship, empathy, consciousness, social awareness, emotional and spiritual intelligence and responsible leadership. Of course, these are harder to measure, but not impossible, and they are certainly needed. Moreover, these attributes may contribute to long-term employability and students' performance, with the rapid changes in the job market.

An academic with a personal impact purpose might have a different teaching philosophy: 'by the end of this course my students will be inspired to help/cure/teach/lead others and in the next few years will continue to use the knowledge gained in this class to better humanity.' A purpose-driven university could measure its teaching quality not by what students are taught, but by how these students apply the knowledge to address societal issues. As Sharma (2015, p. 400) explains:

> Universities can help in providing with the new knowledge and skills needed to meet the challenges of sustainable development in a community, in raising public awareness and providing preconditions for informed decision-making, responsible behavior and consumer choice. [...] Another role that universities may play is in the building of new institutions of civil society, in developing new cultural values, and in training and socializing people of new social era.

Genuine Service, Engagement and Citizenship

In addition to research and teaching, academic staff are usually expected to contribute to their department, academic institution and campus life, in what is often captured under 'service'. Service could be internally direct towards the university, from participation in graduation ceremonies, through departmental committees, to leading administrative roles. This also includes external service, such as 'service to the profession': peer reviewing, organising academic conferences and sitting on the editorial board of academic journals.

Some universities also include good organisational citizenship in 'service': employees exerting efforts to support one another, mentoring junior staff and volunteering for extra-curricular activities. In addition, service may include some contribution to the community, be it an activity organised by the university or the individual employee.

However, service can be much more impactful and holistic than all the above combined. Purpose-driven people ask themselves:

> How can I use my role, knowledge, talent, skills and networks to significantly impact on the world? How can I use who I am, what I know and what I do to change the lives of the largest amount of people possible or at least create the deepest change in several lives?

The purpose-driven university, on the other hand, needs to ask:

> Are we supporting our academic and professional staff enough in their search for purpose? Are we pressuring them to publish at the cost of giving up their passion, good citizenship behaviour and ability to create an impact?

In a purpose-driven university, true service and impact are not only encouraged but they are also recognised and measured. The more people on campus engage in such behaviour, the greater the collective impact is. These outcomes can be measured as part of the university's social impact and become a component in its narrative of change.

Every university has staff working or aiming to work on purpose-driven and impactful work. Every purpose-driven university needs to encourage them to do so, providing them with the required time and recognition to achieve these goals.

Impact-based Promotion

Academic promotion aims to capture the achievements and impact of an applicant in the areas of research, teaching and service. Most academics are highly motivated to work hard and achieve promotion to a full professorship. As it captures all aspects of scholarship (Boyer, 1990), the academic promotion process can be used to exemplify and demonstrate the way that the purpose-driven university works.

First, promotion should be based on all aspects of scholarship, not just on research. The 'publish or perish' approach pressures young academics, leads to a strong sense of competitiveness and possibly to low levels of organisational citizenship behaviour. This pressure can create resentment towards other aspects of scholarship, such as teaching and service, and teaching quality and impactful service may suffer as a result. This does not mean that universities need to choose between being research-led or purpose-driven. Instead, it implies that a holistic and balanced approach is critical.

Universities can then adopt a more holistic approach to promotion. Using Boyer's (1990, 1996) framework, with at least four aspects of scholarship and the inclusion of integration and application, can help to achieve this goal. A promotion based on leadership, service and impact is also an essential milestone on this journey.

Macquarie University in Australia, my university, established a new approach to promotion in 2017. Using Boyer's framework together with a fifth criterion, 'leadership and citizenship', applicants assess themselves on each aspect of scholarship. It engaged many people in reflective practice and understanding that their work needs to be integrative, applied and impactful. It encouraged many more women to apply for a promotion, as some of the criteria related to what females tend to do in academia (see Misra et al., 2011). While it is not perfect and it may take a few years to see the full impact of these changes on the promotion process, it may lead to more impactful research and teaching and to a purpose-driven university.

Imperative Questions to Ask

(1) *What are the implications of being ethical for our university?* A purpose-driven and responsible university should reflect on the ethical approach upon which it manages the institution. It then needs to examine various aspects of the organisation's identity, actions and intentions, to detect potential ethical questions and dilemmas. It is crucial to identify and address ethical ambiguities which could lead to unethical behaviour and corruption and address them in advance.

(2) *What would it mean to adopt a holistic approach?* Mapping all the university's activities, from teaching and research to facilities and procurement, could assist the organisation in finding opportunities to make a momentous contribution to the community and the environment in every aspect of the university's work. One noteworthy way of doing this is by aligning various aspects of the university's work with the SDGs. A holistic approach requires more time, effort and resources than ad hoc or sporadic acts of contribution, but it is the most effective way to create impact and generate trust.

(3) *How can we shift from creating less harm to making a real contribution to the environment?* The recent discourse on sustainability in the business sector and elsewhere is about shifting the idea that sustainability is about doing less harm. Examining sustainability in numerous higher education institutions, it seems that many universities focus on creating less harm: less waste, less energy consumption and fewer carbon emissions. These are all necessary, but it may be time to progress to possible contribution.

Climate change scholars and university engineering professors originate solutions, often in partnerships. There is more work to be done on sharing the story of the academic contribution to sustainable development beyond less harm.

References

Anigma, S. (2016). *Scholarship of engagement*. Corvallis, OR: Oregon State University. Retrieved from www.blogs.oregonstate.edu/engage/2016/03/14/scholarship-of-engagement

Ashwin, P. (2015). *Five ways universities have already changed in the 21st century*. World Economic Forum. Retrieved from www.weforum.org/agenda/2015/05/5-ways-universities-have-already-changed-in-the-21st-century

Boyer, E. L. (1990). *Scholarship reconsidered: Priorities of the professoriate*. Lawrenceville, NJ: Princeton University Press.

Boyer, E. L. (1996). The scholarship of engagement. *Journal of Public Service and Outreach*, *1*(1), 11–20.

Brundtland, G. H. (1987). *Report of the world commission on environment and development: 'Our common future'*. New York, NY: The United Nations.

Crane, A. (2019). *Negative impact: Is it possible to manage potentially harmful research findings?* Retrieved from www.blogs.lse.ac.uk/impactofsocialsciences/2019/04/03/negative-impact-is-it-possible-to-manage-potentially-harmful-research-findings

Hart, D. D., Buizer, J. L., Foley, J. A., Gilbert, L. E., Graumlich, L. J., Kapuscinski, A. R., & Silka, L. (2016). Mobilizing the power of higher education to tackle the grand challenge of sustainability: Lessons from novel initiatives. *Elementa: Science of the Anthropocene*, *4*.

Harty, D., & Stone, R. (2018). *More universities looking to put ESG stamp on billion-dollar endowment funds*. S&P Global. Retrieved from www.spglobal.com/marketintelligence/en/news-insights/trending/q0ww2aae7sa4vvn5zrqu4g2

Haski-Leventhal, D. (2018). *Strategic corporate social responsibility: Tools and theories for responsible management*. London: SAGE.

Hovmöller, E. E. (2019). *How universities can integrate SDGs into higher education*. University World News. Retrieved from www.universityworldnews.com/post.php?story=20190405155329231

Levi, L., & Rothstein, B. (2018). Universities must lead on sustainable development goals. *University World News*. Retrieved from www.universityworldnews.com/post.php?story=20181106131352348

Mackey, J., & Sisodia, R. (2014). *Conscious capitalism*. Boston, MA: Harvard Business Review Press.

Matten, D., & Moon, J. (2008). 'Implicit' and 'explicit' CSR: A conceptual framework for a comparative understanding of corporate social responsibility. *Academy of Management Review*, *33*(2), 404–424.

Milat, A. J., Bauman, A. E., & Redman, S. (2015). A narrative review of research impact assessment models and methods. *Health Research Policy and Systems*, *13*(1), 18.

Misra, J., Lundquist, J. H., Holmes, E., & Agiomavritis, S. (2011). The ivory ceiling of service work. *Academe*, *97*(1), 22–26.

People and Planet. (2019). *University league*. Retrieved from www.peopleandplanet.org/university-league

SDSN. (2017). *Getting started with the SDGs in universities: A guide for universities, higher education institutions, and the academic sector*. Retrieved from www.ap-unsdsn.org/wp-content/uploads/University-SDG-Guide_web.pdf

Sharma, R. S. (2015). Role of universities in development of civil society and social transformation. In Proceedings of international academic conferences, International Institute of Social and Economic Sciences, Vienna, September.

Simon Fraser University. (2019a). *Simon Fraser University launches 20-year sustainability vision and goals*. Retrieved from www.youtube.com/watch?v=p-c1swxTUd4

Simon Fraser University. (2019b). *Simon Fraser University: Strategic vision*. Retrieved from www.sfu.ca/content/dam/sfu/engage/StrategicVision.pdf

Sinek, S. (2011). *Start with why: How great leaders inspire everyone to take action*. London: Penguin Books.

Smith, K. M., Crookes, E., & Crookes, P. A. (2013). Measuring research 'impact' for academic promotion: Issues from the literature. *Journal of Higher Education Policy and Management, 35*(4), 410–420.

Straub, V. (2019). Let's judge universities for their social impact, not graduate salaries. *The Guardian*. Retrieved from www.theguardian.com/education/2019/jul/30/lets-judge-universities-for-their-social-impact-not-graduate-salaries

Times Higher Education (THE). (2019). *University impact rankings 2019*. Retrieved from www.timeshighereducation.com/rankings/impact/2019/overall#!/page/0/length/25/sort_by/rank/sort_order/asc/cols/undefined

United Nations. (2019). *About the sustainable development goals*. Retrieved from www.un.org/sustainabledevelopment/sustainable-development-goals

University of Gothenburg. (2019). *Vision 2020*. Retrieved from www.gu.se/english/about_the_university/vision

Viefers, S. F., Christie, M. F., & Ferdos, F. (2006). Gender equity in higher education: Why and how? A case study of gender issues in a science faculty. *European Journal of Engineering Education, 31*(1), 15–22.

Werther, W. B., & Chandler, D. (2011). *Strategic corporate social responsibility: Stakeholders in a global environment* (2nd ed.). Thousand Oaks, CA: SAGE.

Weybrecht, G. (2017). *Management education's role in the SDGs isn't limited to providing quality education (SDG4). It is broader and more important than that*. Retrieved from www.primetime.unprme.org/2017/07/03/management-educations-role-in-the-sdgs-isnt-limited-to-providing-quality-education-sdg4-it-is-broader-and-more-important-than-that

Winchester, H. P., & Browning, L. (2015). Gender equality in academia: A critical reflection. *Journal of Higher Education Policy and Management, 37*(3), 269–281.

Chapter 4

Leading Universities towards Purpose: The Role of University Leadership

President Amy Gutmann: Leading Penn towards Impact

As the daughter of an immigrant who escaped from Nazi Germany to Bombay and settled in the USA after World War II, Amy Gutmann presents an outstanding example of purposeful leadership. She has been the president of the Ivy League University of Pennsylvania (Penn) since 2004, and in these past 15 years has managed to lead large-scale organisational and social change. In an interview for Women's Way (2017), Professor Gutmann said:

> I was the first in my family to attend college, and although I excelled in high school, I had no insight into how I could possibly afford a first-rate college education. It wasn't until our family doctor urged me to explore the Ivy League, and explained the availability of financial aid, that I even considered applying to Radcliffe (now Harvard), where I eventually enrolled. Education has opened every door for me, and I am committed to being a force for opening doors for others.

Defining her purpose and the purpose of Penn as a force for opening doors, Gutmann led the University to become the nation's largest university offering an all-grant financial aid policy. This policy helps to meet the full needs of undergraduate students. The number of students from low-income, middle-income and first-generation college families has more than doubled since 2004 when Gutmann was appointed president. She has led successful fundraising campaigns amounting to hundreds of millions of US dollars, including the 'Penn First Plus' initiative, targeted to support first-generation, low-income students.

Professor Gutmann is the eighth president of the University of Pennsylvania. She is Christopher H. Browne Distinguished Professor of Political Science, an award-winning political theorist and the author of 16 books and numerous articles. With a contract to serve as president until 2022, Gutmann will be the longest-serving president in the history of Penn. In 2011, *Newsweek* listed her as one of the 150 Women Who Shake the World. Moving from the position of the Provost at

Princeton University, after 27 years, to Penn, was purpose-led: 'It was an opportunity for me to make the maximal difference in people's lives.'

Penn is located at the heart of West Philadelphia, one of the most economically depressed areas in an already depressed city and state. In the 1950s and 1960s, Penn played a negative role in its community, dislocating many poor, mostly black, residents with its property expansion. However, faced with a growing crime problem in the 1980s and 1990s, Penn decided to invest massively in its local community, including in affordable housing, public schools, the local retail strip and economic inclusion strategies (Firth, 2018). Today, thousands of Penn students volunteer in West Philadelphia, either through direct community service or through academic service-learning courses.

In one of her keynote addresses, Gutmann (2011) asked: what makes a university education worthwhile? She had several answers to this question, with a focus on what she called 'contribution':

> The third aim of a university education: maximizing the social contribution of universities based on our core competencies. [...] Universities are engines of both individual empowerment and social progress. The very same creative understanding that empowers individuals to lead productive lives as citizens and professionals also generates social progress. [...] Universities can and should be institutional models of environmental sustainability in the way we build and maintain our campuses.

Penn can set an example of a purpose-driven university through its vision for 2020 – Penn Compact 2020, which focuses on inclusion, innovation and impact ('effecting potent positive impact in our neighborhoods, nation and the world ... are the cornerstones of Penn education'). To achieve these social goals, Penn has many social initiatives, such as the Netter Center for Community Partnerships. The Netter Center is Penn's 'primary vehicle for bringing to bear the broad range of human knowledge needed to solve the complex, comprehensive, and interconnected problems of the American city so that West Philadelphia, Philadelphia, the University itself, and society benefit'. Penn academics are involved in delivering education and engagement to non-university students from greater Philadelphia and creating social impact.

President Gutmann demonstrates that a combination of a purpose-driven leader, institution, staff and students can create a transformational university whose impact can be seen far beyond the institutional boundaries.

Introduction

Universities' leaders have an immense role to play in creating a purpose-driven university and a substantial impact on society and the world. By university leadership, we refer both to formal leaders (e.g. presidents, chancellors, vice chancellors, deans, heads of schools and directors) and informal leaders in the shape of students and staff who strive to lead change in the university and the community. However, while a higher education institution can create its purpose without the support of formal leadership, the process will take longer and will be more challenging to achieve.

Before we embark on a discussion of purpose-driven leadership, it is essential to use a shared definition of this term. Being one of the most researched topics in management and organisational behaviour, leadership has hundreds of definitions, approaches and theories. One of these definitions describes leadership as 'a process of social influence in which one person can enlist the aid and support of others in the accomplishment of a common task' (Chemers, 2000, p. 27). Therefore, the scope of leadership can be outlined by the nature of these 'common tasks': Are they focused on a group, the organisation or society? While a transactional leader only focuses on the task of serving one's organisation, a purpose-driven leader has a broader task of serving the community. Subsequently, the organisation becomes the means to the end instead of the end itself.

We will, therefore, dedicate this chapter to the role of academic and university leaders in leading a purpose-driven university. We will begin by examining the literature of university leadership. This will be followed by an in-depth discussion of purpose-driven leadership, and how it includes a vision, service, consciousness, shared power and inspiration. As such, this chapter will utilise various ideas, concepts and theories from the leadership literature, including transformational leadership, servant leadership, shared leadership and conscious leadership.

Effective University Leadership

Research shows that university leadership is fundamentally different from leadership in other contexts, and demands additional competencies (Spendlove, 2007). Changes facing higher education from increased government, student and community demands are resulting in a greater focus on leadership within universities (Jones, Harvey, Lefoe, & Ryland, 2014). To remain viable, universities must build their capacity to respond promptly, positively and wisely to these increasing demands and challenges (Fullan, 1993). There is ample evidence of the criticality of the presence of effective and capable leaders to productivity, morale and the success of change in universities (Scott, Coates, & Anderson, 2008).

The effective leadership and management of universities is a crucial issue for policymakers, university staff and the leaders themselves (Spendlove, 2007). University leaders have a central role in ensuring that their institutions not only survive but thrive in the new transnational, IT-enabled, volatile and competitive environment (Scott et al., 2008). Jones et al. (2014) argued that what is needed is a new approach to university leadership that goes beyond individual control and management bureaucracy to embrace more sharing and collaboration.

The emerging literature on leadership in higher education indicates that successful universities require leaders with a unique set of capabilities. Spendlove (2007) found that academic credibility (a robust research profile) and experience of university life were crucial to effective leadership in higher education. People skills, including the ability to communicate and negotiate with others, were also necessary. However, most universities in this study had no systematic approach for either identifying or developing leadership skills. Scott et al. (2008) also demonstrated that university leaders had to lead by example and be a positive role model. Bryman (2007) showed that effective leaders in higher education led with a vision and with alignment around a cause. Effective leaders did more than merely set out a direction for their organisation or department – they also made sure that the unit was prepared for the direction the leader had set in motion. They did so with empathy, consideration, trust, warmth and mutual respect between leader and followers. They shared their leadership role, and acted as a credible role model, while creating a positive and collegial work atmosphere.

Against this backdrop, a conclusion may emerge that leaders in higher education may be more effective if they lead with a transformational vision, with a sense of calling, through shared leadership and high levels of emotional intelligence and consciousness. Most importantly, they must lead with a direction and a cause – in other words, with a purpose.

Purpose-Driven Leadership

Purpose-driven leadership inspires, enables and cultivates action in others, in order to create and achieve an aspirational reason for being. A purpose-driven leader sees both their personal life and organisational power as an opportunity to serve and make a difference in other people's lives. Such a leader is not only driven by purpose but also leads in an inclusive way that enables others to find their own purpose. Purpose-driven leaders use their formal role to create a positive impact and enable others to do the same. This is important because it can help to serve the world, the organisation and the individuals better. It can lead to a sense of meaningfulness, wellbeing and resilience.

Some leaders are naturally purpose-driven, whereas others need to discover a way to live a purposeful life. There is no one purpose that a person needs to discover. Rather, one can live a purposeful life by connecting their talent, joy and impact. Leaders can become more purpose-driven by developing their emotional intelligence and empathy, their spiritual intelligence, compassion, self-transcendent values and reflective practice (among other skills and competencies). In the same vein, a purpose-driven leader helps to create a purpose-driven organisation by discovering what the organisational strengths are, and by harnessing the organisation's power, resources and people to create a positive impact in the world.

In a remarkable TED talk, orchestra conductor Benjamin Zander shares how, at the age of 45, he realised that the conductor makes no sound but 'depends for his power on his ability to make other people powerful'. This was a life-changing insight, which led him to redefine his role and the role of a leader as one of awakening possibilities in others. 'And you know you are doing this', he added, 'if their eyes are shining'. Zander continues to say that if their eyes are not shining, one must ask: 'whom am I being that my players'/employees' eyes are not shining? What kind of a leader am I, that people's eyes around me are not shining?'

The purpose-driven leader evokes possibilities in others and ignites the search for a more purposeful life, which is what lights their inner fire. In an organisation, such as a university, this can be contagious. Working with many passionate and purposeful people around us can make us engaged and may replace the notion of 'work' with the notion of purpose.

Leading with Purpose, Transforming with Vision

Leaders have the power to enhance the meaningfulness of work by expressing the organisation's ultimate goals and aspirations (Gioia & Chittipeddi, 1991; Shamir, House, & Arthur, 1993). As such, the essence of leadership is strongly tied to purpose. An effective leader never leads followers with no specific goal. The goal may be to maximise shareholder value or increase the university's ranking, but it can also be an impact purpose to be a force for positive change.

Consequently, leading with a purpose implies leading with a vision. A higher purpose, both personally and organisationally, is an aspirational reason to live and a notion that people are part of something bigger than themselves. A purpose-driven leader can play a vital role in seeing what the potential impact can do for the world and the organisation and in portraying this vision to others, so they too can mentally see it.

As discussed in Chapter 1, a strong and shared vision can be crucial for the success and impact of universities all around the world. A compelling vision and purpose are what make academic leaders stand out. In an article on the 20 leading college presidents in the USA (The Best Schools, 2019), it was elucidated:

> The college and university presidents on this list are all colorful personalities who not only lead their institutions effectively but do so with a panache and verve that excites their campus community. These are presidents with intriguing life stories, with impressive records of accomplishment, with charisma and vision that inspire faculty, staff, and students to strive for new heights.

University leaders were included on the list of best presidents due to their ability to lead with courage, purpose and a strong vision.

Back in 1976, Reverend Theodore Hesburgh, the then president of the University of Notre Dame for 25 years, spoke in his annual address about the role of vision in university leadership:

> This assumes, of course, that the president does have a clear vision for the institution, a vision that is educationally sound and integral, given the available resources. [...] Whatever else he is clear and enthusiastic about, the president must most of all elaborate his specific vision, rethink it as times change, perfect it as he learns from experience or develops new resources. He may be the best administrator in the world, but without a clear and bright

and, yes, beautiful vision, he is leading nowhere. Without a vision, the people perish. Each president will have his own style, no matter, but beyond all style must be substance. [...] He will simply lose the faculty and he will be unable to lead them anywhere, certainly not to the promised land.

Today, while we would use a less gender-discriminatory language, his words still echo truth: without a strong vision, a leader is just an administrator.

The concept of **transformational leadership** is useful to shed light on the importance of a robust vision in leadership, including purpose-driven. While the concept of transformational leadership has been vastly used since the 1970s to effectively lead organisations in general, some of its components can be applied to leaders who make a genuine difference in the world (Groves & LaRocca, 2011). Transformational leadership details how leaders change organisations by creating, communicating and modelling a vision for the organisation and by inspiring employees to strive towards this vision (Bass, 1985; Burns, 1978). While transactional leadership relies on offering tangible rewards and exchange to influence people's behaviour, transformational leaders understand that people are also purpose-driven and vision-driven and tap into their higher purpose.

As such, this leadership style is associated with being a moral agent, raising others to higher levels of moral consciousness and creating a shared vision and meaning (Angus-Leppan, Metcalf, & Benn, 2010). Transformational leaders can lead to a higher purpose by seeing the possibilities of impact in the near and far future, creating a story of change which is shared with everyone around them, walking the talk with integrity and creating commitment and engagement around this purpose.

Research shows that transformational leadership can help make a difference, motivate employees and create an emotional attachment to the organisation. They inspire people by shifting the focus from the individual to the collective, thus engaging employees through a vision for a higher purpose (Waldman, Siegel, & Javidan, 2006). It is, therefore, an essential part of leading a purpose-driven university.

In the Service of Others

Purpose-driven university leaders are not just focused on their power and success, but they are also dedicated to others' success and to the way in which the success of their university can be used to serve others. This strong sense of service can help university leaders to define the university's vision and purpose collectively.

If purpose is defined as impact and service, to be a purpose-driven leader implies being a servant-leader. Servant leadership focuses on serving others due to a sense of calling and higher purpose. As Robert Greenleaf (1970, p. 7) explained:

> The servant-leader is a servant first. It begins with the natural feeling that one wants to serve, to serve first. Then conscious choice brings one to aspire to lead. That person is sharply different from one who is a leader first, perhaps because of the

need to assuage an unusual power drive or to acquire material possessions. The leader-first and the servant-first are two extreme types. Between them, there are shadings and blends that are part of the infinite variety of human nature.

Servant leadership is based on the view that leadership is a duty, instead of an entitlement, a reward or an achievement. Traditional leadership generally involves the accumulation and exercise of power by one at the 'top of the pyramid'. In contrast, the servant-leader shares power, puts the needs of others first and helps people develop and perform as highly as possible. Consequently, leaders are to serve their country, society, organisation, employees and stakeholders. To paraphrase Kennedy, 'ask not what others can do for you, but how you may serve others'.

President Barack Obama volunteered on the eve of his Inauguration Day and called people to also use this day, Martin Luther King Day, to serve. He spoke about service and purpose in his commencement address at Morehouse College (Obama, 2016), encouraging the new graduates to do the same:

> So, yes, go get that law degree. But if you do, ask yourself if the only option is to defend the rich and the powerful, or if you can also find some time to defend the powerless. Sure, go get your MBA, or start that business. [...] But ask yourselves what broader purpose your business might serve, in putting people to work, or transforming a neighbourhood. The most successful CEOs I know didn't start out intent just on making money – rather, they had a vision of how their product or service would change things, and the money followed.

Servant-leaders in higher education institutions can lead by example, demonstrating how they use their position of power to serve the university and the community in which it operates. The opening case of President Amy Gutmann exemplifies this well. More importantly, such academic leaders harness the power of the entire university to serve, encourage service in all academic and professional staff and the students as well and recognise such service in celebrating the individuals who serve, and the collective.

Spears (2002) detailed the various attributes of the servant-leader, such as listening, empathy, healing, awareness and persuasion. However, the first attribute on this list is a sense of calling and a higher purpose because servant-leaders have a strong sense of purpose and are willing to sacrifice themselves for others. This calling to serve is deeply rooted and values-based, and these leaders desire to pursue opportunities to make a difference and to impact the lives of others instead of seeking their own gain.

Subsequently, purposefulness and service are strongly connected. One cannot be a servant-leader without a clear impact purpose. One cannot be a purpose-driven leader, leading a purpose-driven university, without the servant-leader's humbleness and desire to serve others. This can be even more challenging to people in a position of considerable power, such as university presidents, as people tend to attribute success to themselves. It may require hard and reflective work to let go of the sense of entitlement and learn to be a humbler person of service.

High Levels of Consciousness

In addition to leading with a purpose and vision for the service of others, purpose-driven leaders act with a high level of consciousness. Consciousness relates to a person's state of awareness of the self, others and the world around them. Based on people's values and ethos, they can develop high levels of consciousness and an empathetic view of the world and use their role to address social issues. As higher levels of consciousness are related to self-awareness as well, conscious leaders are more authentic.

The idea of conscious leadership was developed in the context of conscious capitalism (see Chapter 3 under 'Conscious Universities'). It is part of the four tenets of a conscious business, all of which are interconnected. A conscious leader leads with a higher purpose, develops a conscious culture in the organisation and integrates all stakeholders so that together this higher purpose can be achieved.

Research shows a relationship between consciousness development, better leadership performance and positive organisational outcomes (Vincent, Denson, & Ward, 2015). The level of consciousness that leaders possess has a significant impact on their ability to navigate uncertainty, deal with complex issues, lead change and successfully promote innovation.

Conscious leadership brings an innovative approach to the leadership literature, as it integrates the best from authentic, transformational and servant leadership theories with the need for personal change. University leaders, who usually have a high IQ, can become conscious leaders by also developing their emotional intelligence (EQ) and spiritual intelligence (SQ). Both EQ and SQ can help leaders to become more empathetically aware of the world and of the ways universities may serve it.

EQ has been defined as 'the ability to carry out accurate reasoning about emotions and the ability to use emotions and emotional knowledge to enhance thought' (Mayer, Salovey, & Caruso, 2008, p. 507). This concept gained popularity in the 1990s, when Daniel Goleman presented it in his book *Emotional Intelligence: Why It Can Matter More Than IQ* (1995). Since then, much research has been done on the concept and emerging measures of EQ have been developed. The research shows that EQ is related not only to better personal relationships, but also to better management, organisational performance and even to higher performance among academics (Mayer et al., 2008).

In his later book, *Working with Emotional Intelligence* (1998), Goleman applied EQ to the workplace, arguing that the emotionally intelligent worker is skilled in two key areas: personal competence (managing oneself) and social competence (managing relationships). In his more recent book, *Force for Good* (2015), Goleman combines his ideas with the thoughts of the Dalai Lama, to discuss how one can combine EQ with purpose. EQ enables higher levels of compassion which is necessary for igniting the desire to help and make a difference. Consider how many universities focus on EQ and compassion as key graduate capabilities, and how important this could be for us to address society's greatest issues.

Similarly, the concept SQ is now becoming accepted and relevant. Developed by Zohar (Zohar, 2005; Zohar & Marshall, 2001) and others, SQ is defined as the intelligence with which we solve issues around meaning and value, and through which we place our lives (including study and work) in a wide, rich, meaning-giving context. SQ is about living a meaningful life through a higher purpose, through a search for meaning and a sense of belonging to something greater than ourselves. Signs of high SQ include an awareness and consciousness of the self and of others, modesty and an access to energies that come from something beyond the ego, beyond just us and our day-to-day concerns.

The definition of SQ has nothing to do with religion, which often confines believers to one truth. Instead, SQ opens endless possibilities for living according to our individual values in connection with others. The dictionary definition (Merriam Webster, 2019) of spirit is an animating or vital principle held to give life to physical organisms, and, as such, spiritual means to be relating to, consisting of or affecting the spirit. SQ is therefore about what gives us life, not just in the physical sense, but in the emotional, spiritual and relational sense as well.

Zohar (2005) explained that for organisations, business or others, to succeed they need all three capitals: financial capital, social capital and spiritual capital. The immense focus on material and financial capital has led us to short-term thinking and to the crisis humanity is facing today. Social capital, on the other hand, includes trust, empathy and commitment to the health of the community. Spiritual capital reflects what we exist for, believe in, aspire to be and take responsibility for. Spiritual capital is a new paradigm that requires a radical change in the philosophical foundations and practices of leadership. Spiritual capital refers to the power a leader can unleash in individuals and organisations by evoking people's deepest meanings, values and purposes. Leaders need to use all three types of intelligence (IQ, EQ and SQ) to develop the three types of capital and lead to higher levels of success, purpose, impact and meaning. The secret of conscious leadership is the ability to inspire people, to give them a sense of something worth struggling for.

In one of our recent studies (not yet published), we examined the life stories of business leaders and social entrepreneurs who exhibit high levels of consciousness. What emerged was a journey towards conscious leadership which typically included: (1) the cultivation of SQ (self-development); (2) eye-opening experiences (external triggers); (3) meaningful encounters with other conscious leaders (relational power); and (4) the ability to heal, both oneself and others (changing patterns and behaviours). Many people (and leaders) face difficulties and adversities, but having a high EQ and IQ creates an ability to heal which is why such leaders are able to show high awareness of and compassion for the self and others.

> **Box 4.1. Juliet V. García: A Conscious University Leader**
>
> Juliet Villarreal García is the senior adviser to the chancellor for community, national and global engagement at the University of Texas System. Previously, she served as president of the University of Texas at Brownsville, a position she held for 22 years. García became the first Mexican American woman to head a college or university when she was named president of Texas Southmost College in 1986, at the young age of 37. *Time* magazine listed her as one of the Top 10 College Presidents in the USA in 2009 and she was inducted into the Texas Women's Hall of Fame for Lifetime Achievement in Education.
>
> She is the daughter of a migrant family from Mexico, whose father worked hard as a janitor, putting a dollar to dollar to send his children to college, after García's mother died at a young age. Her difficult early experiences and her ability to develop her resilience made her a conscious leader.
>
> In her TED talk from 2018, García shares how she was working hard to raise 1 million dollars, to be matched with another 2 million, providing thousands of scholarships for underprivileged students. People from all around the community, including children, hardworking migrants and big foundations, helped her achieve this goal. However, it was a woman who walked many blocks with two babies to come and meet her and donate $5 that stayed with her the most. Knowing that this woman must have needed this money more than the college, she asked her: 'Why are you giving me this money?' And the woman replied: 'Because it is the only hope that I have for my children.' García took the money and achieved her goal. 'This lady taught me that we do this work because it gives hope. Because it changes lives. ... Working together with communities, working with each other, that matters. Spend your life doing work that matters.'

Shared Leadership

Purpose-driven leaders who act from a higher purpose and aim to serve others never do so alone. When a leader keeps all the power to himself/herself, it contradicts the very essence of being a purpose-driven leader. Purpose-driven leadership is always shared leadership, as we all work together to achieve a collective goal, beyond the organisational goal.

Shared leadership is based on the notion that nearly every person in the organisation is capable of sharing the responsibility of leading, at least to some extent, in nearly all types of organisational circumstances (Pearce & Conger, 2003). All leadership is shared leadership; it is simply a matter of degree, and, at its highest level, all the social actors in an organisation or a team are involved in the process of leading one another towards a shared purpose (Pearce, Wassenaar, & Manz, 2014). Shared leadership flourishes when formal leaders delegate power and encourage employees to take initiative and risks without fear of failure.

Shared leadership suggests that leadership is plural, not singular. Jones et al. (2014) argued that shared and distributed leadership is what contributes to effective leadership in higher education, particularly in times of change. In higher education institutions, there could be many academics, professional staff and even students who hold the knowledge, capabilities and passion to help lead in certain areas. All these people might help to shape the future of our university, its purpose and its shared narrative of impact. Students and staff can become powerful change agents and help lead and facilitate this change by working with all stakeholders to achieve the vision and purpose of the university. Doing so might lead to a collaborative rather than an internally competitive culture, particularly when a clear purpose is shared by everyone. This, in turn, will lead to high levels of organisational citizenship behaviour that improve the performance and wellbeing of employees, their peers and the entire organisation. Shared purpose-driven leadership is key to achieving all these imperative goals.

In summary, a purpose-driven university requires leaders, both formal and informal, who lead with a higher purpose. They do so with a strong vision; a sense of calling and service; high levels of consciousness, EQ and SQ; and the ability to share responsibility with others. Integrating these leadership styles and attributes is what can help a university change its focus and direction to become a force for good in the community and in the world.

Imperative Questions to Ask

(1) *What kind of leader would best suit our university?* Universities often search the globe in pursuit of presidents, vice chancellors and even deans. Each such search begins with a long list of selection criteria, usually about the part the person has played in success, and their competencies and ability to create high levels of success. For a purpose-driven university, these criteria will likely differ. Such universities will search for leaders with high levels of purpose, consciousness, EQ, SQ and a vision to better humanity. The nature of a university's leaders and the type of search criteria used in recruiting new ones can indicate the level of purposefulness of that university and its commitment to being best for the world.

(2) *How do we encourage informal leadership for purpose?* As purpose driven leadership is not only carried by the people at the top with formal titles, it is important to cultivate such leadership among other people in the university who are capable and motivated. It is important to ask what can be done to share the narrative of a purpose-driven university and to make it a shared goal for as many people as possible. As many individuals work independently on purpose-related initiatives, each university needs to ask: How can we weave connections, bring down silos and empower people to co-lead towards the shared purpose?

References

Angus-Leppan, T., Metcalf, L., & Benn, S. (2010). Leadership styles and CSR practice: An examination of sensemaking, institutional drivers and CSR leadership. *Journal of Business Ethics, 93*(2), 189–213.

Bass, B. M. (1985). *Leadership and performance beyond expectations.* New York, NY: Free Press.

Bryman, A. (2007). Effective leadership in higher education: A literature review. *Studies in Higher Education, 32*(6), 693–710.

Burns, J. M. (1978). *Leadership.* New York, NY: Harper & Row.

Chemers, M. M. (2000). Leadership research and theory: A functional integration. *Group Dynamics: Theory, Research, and Practice, 4*(1), 27–43.

Firth, V. (2018). *Social impact: A framework for critically engaged universities.* Retrieved from www.engagementaustralia.org.au/wp-content/uploads/2018/12/Article-7_TRANSFORM-No-1-2018_Social-Impact-A-Framework-for-Critically-Engaged-Universities.pdf

Fullan, M. (1993). *Change forces: Probing the depths of educational reform.* London: Falmer Press.

Gioia, D. A., & Chittipeddi, K. (1991). Sensemaking and sensegiving in strategic change initiation. *Strategic Management Journal, 12*(6), 433–448.

Goleman, D. (1995). *Emotional intelligence: Why it can matter more than IQ.* New York, NY: Bantam.

Goleman, D. (1998). *Working with emotional intelligence.* New York, NY: Bantam.

Goleman, D. with the Dalai Lama (2015). *Force for good.* New York, NY: Bantam.

Greenleaf, R. (1970). *The servant as leader.* New York, NY: Paulist Press.

Groves, K. S., & LaRocca, M. A. (2011). An empirical study of leader ethical values, transformational and transactional leadership, and follower attitudes toward corporate social responsibility. *Journal of Business Ethics, 103*(4), 511–528.

Gutmann, A. (2011). *What makes a university education worthwhile?* Retrieved from www.president.upenn.edu/meet-president/what-makes-university-education-worthwhile

Jones, S., Harvey, M., Lefoe, G., & Ryland, K. (2014). Synthesising theory and practice: Distributed leadership in higher education. *Educational Management Administration & Leadership, 42*(5), 603–619.

Mayer, J. D., Salovey, P., & Caruso, D. R. (2008). Emotional intelligence: New ability or eclectic traits? *American Psychologist, 63*(6), 503.

Merriam Webster. (2019). *Spirit.* Retrieved from www.merriam-webster.com/dictionary/spirit

Obama, B. (2016). *President Obama's commencement address at Morehouse College.* Retrieved from www.time.com/4341712/obama-commencement-speech-transcript-morehouse-college/

Pearce, C. L., & Conger, J. A. (2003). *Shared leadership: Reframing the hows and whys of leadership.* Thousand Oaks, CA: SAGE.

Pearce, C. L., Wassenaar, C. L., & Manz, C. C. (2014). Is shared leadership the key to responsible leadership?. *Academy of Management Perspectives, 28*(3), 275–288.

Scott, G., Coates, H., & Anderson, M. (2008). *Learning leaders in times of change: Academic leadership capabilities for Australian higher education.* Sydney, NSW: University of Western Sydney and Australian Council for Educational Research.

Shamir, B., House, R. J., & Arthur, M. B. (1993). The motivational effects of charismatic leadership: A self-concept based theory. *Organization Science*, *4*(4), 577–594.

Spears, L. C. (2002). Tracing the past, present, and future of servant-leadership. In L. C. Spears & M. Lawrence (Eds), *Focus on leadership: Servant-leadership for the twenty-first century* (pp. 1–16). New York, NY: Wiley.

Spendlove, M. (2007). Competencies for effective leadership in higher education. *International Journal of Educational Management*, *21*(5), 407–417.

The Best Schools. (2019). *The 20 most interesting college presidents*. Retrieved from www.thebestschools.org/features/most-interesting-college-presidents

Vincent, N., Denson, L., & Ward, L. (2015). Triggers, timing and type: Exploring developmental readiness and the experience of consciousness transformation in graduates of Australian community leadership programs. *Journal of Adult Development*, *22*(4), 183–205.

Waldman, D. A., Siegel, D. S., & Javidan, M. (2006). Components of CEO transformational leadership and corporate social responsibility. *Journal of Management Studies*, *43*(8), 1703–1725.

Women's Way. (2017). *A powerful voice for all: Interview with Dr. Amy Gutmann*. Retrieved from www.womensway.org/a-powerful-voice-for-all-interview-with-dr-amy-gutmann

Zohar, D. (2005). Spiritually intelligent leadership. *Leader to Leader*, *38*, 45–51.

Zohar, D., & Marshall, I. (2001). *SQ: Connecting with our spiritual intelligence*. New York, NY: Bloomsbury Publishing.

Chapter 5

Purpose-related Stakeholders

The Stakeholder Approach at Oxford University

The University of Oxford is one of the oldest universities in the world, with evidence of teaching commencing in 1096, and one of the most prestigious. Today, with more than 22,000 students, 13,000 staff and 230,000 alumni around the world, Oxford claims that it is people who make Oxford an internationally renowned university. With this emphasis on the various people the University affects, it has a noteworthy approach to its stakeholders. Since 2016, it has been led by Professor Louise Richardson in the role of vice chancellor, a position held by a female leader for the first time (Oxford, 2019).

Oxford governance is based not on one executive leader, but on its Congregation, a sovereign body of the University which acts as its 'parliament'. With over 5000 members (including academic staff; heads and other members of governing bodies of colleges; and senior research, computing, library and administrative staff), the Congregation is responsible for approving changes to the University's statutes and regulations; considering major policy issues; and electing members to Council and other University bodies, and approving the appointment of the vice chancellor.

Oxford's vision is set out in its strategic plan for 2018–23, listing the stakeholders of the University and detailing the way in which it integrates them into its strategy (Oxford, 2018):

> We will work as one Oxford bringing together our staff, students and alumni, our colleges, faculties, departments and divisions to provide world-class research and education. We will do this in ways which benefit society on a local, regional, national and global scale. We will build on the University's long-standing traditions of independent scholarship and academic freedom while fostering a culture in which innovation and collaboration play an important role.
>
> We are committed to equality of opportunity, to engendering inclusivity, and to supporting staff and student wellbeing, ensuring that the very best students and staff can flourish in our community. We believe that a diverse staff and student body strengthens our research and enhances our students' learning.

When it comes to its internal stakeholders (i.e. employees), Oxford has three commitments: to attract, recruit and retain the highest calibre staff; to work towards an increasingly diverse staffing profile; and to support staff in personal and professional development.

In addition, Oxford is committed to working with external stakeholders in the community and the public to exchange knowledge and create an innovative culture. To do this, the University commits to 'work in partnership with public, private, voluntary and commercial organisations, and our alumni'. More specifically, Oxford commits to: (1) work with partners to create a world-class regional innovation ecosystem; (2) build a stronger and more constructive relationship with its local and regional community; (3) engage with the public and policymakers to shape its research and education and to encourage the widest possible use of its research findings and expertise; and (4) maximise the global social, cultural and economic benefit derived from its research and scholarship. To this end, the University states:

> We believe that it is vitally important that the University benefits local citizens. [...] We will continue to provide gateways for public engagement with the research and teaching of the University [...]. We are committed to working in partnership to increase our cultural, societal and economic impact at both local and regional levels.

In addition, the University sees the ecological environment as a major stakeholder and is committed to reducing its carbon emissions by 33% from 2005 to 2020. Oxford publishes related strategies and documents, including its biodiversity strategy, carbon management strategy, sustainable procurement strategy, sustainable transport strategy and water management strategy. To illustrate, as part of its sustainable procurement strategy, Oxford encourages its suppliers to decrease any reliance on non-renewable resources within their production processes; to systematically reduce the use of unsustainable materials; and to reduce the use of virgin materials.

In 2009, Oxford engaged in a mapping exercise of its stakeholders as part of its Research Information Infrastructure project. Based on extensive research, the University defined its stakeholders as 'everyone whose work is directly or indirectly related to research activities or who are interested in them; and who need to access and display research-related information'. In this specific project, the stakeholders included researchers, administrative staff, and strategists and disseminators.

Oxford is not only one of the best universities in the world, leading with research and education, it also demonstrates outstanding social responsibility and stakeholder engagement. Such a stakeholder integration policy and activity help Oxford enhance its reputation in the community and become more purposeful and impactful. This, in turn, also helps Oxford to excel further.

Stakeholder Theory and Purpose-related Stakeholders

Stakeholder theory was developed in the 1980s as a contrast to the wide assumption that companies are only responsible to their shareholders, with the mere responsibility to increase shareholder value. Instead, stakeholder theory (Freeman, 1984) asserted that stakeholders could be any person or a group that affects the organisation or are affected by it achieving its goals. This effect can be both positive and negative, voluntary or involuntary. As such, if a company's goal is to sell as many products and services as possible to maximise its profit, its stakeholders will include employees, consumers, shareholders and suppliers, as the most apparent ones. However, stakeholders also include competitors, the community and the environment, as they too can help or prevent the company from achieving its goals, and they are certainly affected by the same. Stakeholder theory is important because, particularly in business, it helped organisations broaden their range of responsibilities and the entities with whom they need to work. Stakeholder theory was so well accepted because of our social needs and motivations, as it touched our sense of belonging to a tribe.

There are many categorisations of stakeholder groups, particularly for business. These include internal and external, major and minor, and active versus non-active stakeholders. One of my lightbulb moments, which also led me to write this book, was when I read *Conscious Capitalism* (Mackey & Sisodia, 2014) in which the authors discuss major and minor stakeholders. Under major, they listed employees (who they call 'team members'), customers, investors, suppliers, communities and the environment. The minor stakeholders ('outer circle') included competitors, activists, critics, unions, media and government. I was holding this book when it occurred to me that universities are never listed anywhere as a stakeholder, major or minor. It was striking to realise that in all the years of teaching CSR, and in all the numerous classes in which stakeholder groups were listed, none of my students, nor I, had thought of listing universities as a stakeholder of business. Nonetheless, almost every university on the planet has corporate partners, conducts research with companies, offers education and executive education to their future and current employees, and produces research, products, publications, patents and ideas that are often used by the business sector. Is it due to the ignorance of business organisations that higher education institutions are never listed, or is it because we fail to portray our importance to the economy and the community because we are not creating narratives of impact?

In addition to universities being stakeholders of other entities, as organisations, they have their own set of stakeholders. As explained by Simms and Chapleo (2010), while most of the stakeholder literature refers to business and other organisations, there is hardly any literature on universities' stakeholders. These authors explained that some of the existing business stakeholder frameworks will be relevant to universities, but that universities have a unique nature in their operations and responsibilities. As such, universities have a particularly complex stakeholder environment, and the examination of their stakeholder environment and management is pertinent. In this research, stakeholders were identified according to their direct impact on the university (e.g. students, academic staff, funding bodies and governance) and their indirect impact (e.g. taxpayers, not-for-profit organisations, the media).

Conversely, higher education institutions need to go beyond listing and mapping their stakeholders, to focus instead on working with these stakeholders to achieve a common purpose that will position universities as a significant player in this field. A purpose-driven university does not just work with its stakeholders, but it integrates them around a shared purpose, so they become its purpose-related stakeholders.

Presented in *Conscious Capitalism* (Mackey & Sisodia, 2014), stakeholder integration shifts away from stakeholder management and certainly from stakeholder prioritisation. Stakeholder management refers to the way an organisation maps its stakeholders, communicates with them and maintains a good enough relationship so as to minimise the potential detrimental behaviour of these stakeholders. For example, if an organisation does not manage its employees well, they may go on a strike. If a company does not deliver high-quality goods, consumers may stop purchasing them or, in a more extreme scenario, initiate a boycott. Governments may regulate higher education institutions; competitors may obliterate them; and the media can criticise them. Therefore, stakeholder management is often a risk-mitigation approach. In the same vein, stakeholder prioritisation can help an organisation to prioritise stakeholders according to their materiality and allocate time and efforts accordingly. It is not surprising that these exercises lead many businesses to prioritise shareholders far above everyone else and make business decisions accordingly.

Stakeholder integration, on the other hand, shifts away from both these approaches. It does not assume that the organisation is in a power position to 'manage' its stakeholders. The basic definition of management is 'controlling things or people', and no organisation can fully control its stakeholders. Instead, integration means that the organisation involves its stakeholders, maintains a good relationship based on respect and creates mutual benefit and trust. Stakeholder integration shifts away from the 'zero-sum' approach, where there are trade-offs and by which benefiting one stakeholder group implies drawbacks to another. Instead, stakeholder integration suggests a win^6 (i.e. win-win-win-win-win-win) option, whereby all six major stakeholders can benefit.

Stakeholder integration is a more suitable approach in the context of the purpose-driven university. An organisation with a clear purpose does not manage its stakeholders or even integrate them, just for profit and reputation. When there is a well-defined impact purpose, the purpose-related stakeholders gather around a shared commitment and work together to help achieve it. The purpose then becomes the perpetual flame around which all stakeholders can connect, find synergies and work collaboratively.

In a purpose-driven university, the students, academic staff, professional staff, alumni, university leadership, donors, corporate partners, government and the broader community all know the purpose of the university and collaborate (see Fig. 5.1). They do so not because someone manages them, but because they are inspired by the purpose and develop a sense of ownership over it. In the story of Juliet García in Chapter 4, the entire university community and all its stakeholders shared the same purpose of giving hope to young students and their families. This is the reason a woman with no money walked 10 blocks with two babies to give García a five-dollar note – not because she was managed or even asked, but because she shared the same purpose and hope.

Fig. 5.1. University Stakeholders' Map.

This chapter will, therefore, detail the major stakeholder groups of any university to discuss how they might help the university to achieve its purpose. When this happens, a spillover effect occurs, and students, staff and other people start to develop a sense of ownership over the university's purpose, and a notion that by working towards this purpose they too may find their purpose. Consequently, work and education become more meaningful and impactful.

Students: The Most Purpose-Driven Generation

Students comprise one of the most critical stakeholder groups of any university. While some universities are led by research, most of them still deliver higher education and, without the students, this cannot be achieved. This is not only due to tuition fees, but because education requires both educators and students, a sender and a receiver, although meaningful education is usually based on shared learning (Parsell, Spalding, & Bligh, 1998).

Students are also principal stakeholders because they create the backbone of society and the next generation of scholars, managers and teachers. They will occupy vital roles in business, government and not-for-profits, many of which require higher education to succeed. Every academic, from lecturers to full professors, and from tutors to vice chancellors, were all students once.

This generation of students, comprised of millennials (born 1981–1996) and Generation Z (born 1997–2012), is said to be the most purpose-driven generation ever (Leibson, 2018; Odell, 2018). The latest findings from the Pew Research

Centre (2019) reveal that millennials are becoming the world's most influential group in terms of consumer spending growth, sourcing of employees and overall economic prospects. Together with Gen Z, they will be the next cohort of university students and academics, and they may be more purpose-driven than previous generations.

A study I have conducted with business students around the world showed that over 90% of students were willing to sacrifice a portion of their future salary to work for a responsible employer. Furthermore, one in five students are willing to sacrifice over 40% of these salaries (Haski-Leventhal & Pournader, 2017). However, the Deloitte Millennial Survey (2018) found that 75% of millennials believe that most businesses focus on their own agenda, rather than considering wider society. This presents a gap between the students' personal purpose and the perceived lack of purpose of those organisations around them. This also presents an opportunity for employers and universities to attract these generations via a strong impact purpose.

Growing up with climate change as a reality and with access to information like no other generation before them, the new cohorts of students are demanding action. They demand action from governments (see the remarkable example of Swedish teenager Greta Thunberg, who has led millions of students on 'Strike for Climate' marches all over the world). They hold organisations accountable, such as business (running social media smearing campaigns when a business fails to do the right thing) and universities (e.g. Green League, People and Planet).

This generation is actively searching for purpose and for purpose-driven organisations in which to work and study. When an organisation succeeds in communicating its purpose and creating a shared sense of purpose, it will successfully attract younger people. As such, since universities want to attract students, and since most students are now millennials or younger, the conclusion is that universities need to attract them through purpose.

However, this generation is not just interested in finding personal purpose. Young people want to be part of a large-scale purpose through a bigger group or entity, and universities can play this role perfectly. As Mark Zuckerberg, the millennial founder and CEO of Facebook, said in his commencement speech at Harvard University in 2017:

> Today I want to talk about purpose. But I'm not here to give you the standard commencement about finding your purpose. We're millennials. We'll try to do that instinctively. Instead, I'm here to tell you finding your purpose isn't enough. The challenge for our generation is creating a world where everyone has a sense of purpose. [...] Purpose is that sense that we are part of something bigger than ourselves, that we are needed, that we have something better ahead to work for. Purpose is what creates true happiness. [...] But it's not enough to have purpose yourself. You have to create a sense of purpose for others. [...] My hope was never to build a company, but to make an impact.

As such, it is essential not only to communicate the university's purpose with future, current and past students, but also to involve those students in achieving this purpose. A purpose-driven university empowers and enables students to find their purpose and live a purposeful life. My personal story which I shared in the introduction of the book shows that volunteering activities encouraged through the university did not only provide me with a sense of impact and purpose but also created a path to a purpose-driven life and career.

According to Urquilla (2016), students seeking social impact careers often regard business schools as the source for learning opportunities. While business schools can help students develop skills to assist them in working toward the triple bottom line, universities need to extend social impact education into other disciplines. The world needs a variety of leaders, with a range of expertise, committed to the public good in every sector – and universities, as multidisciplinary environments, are uniquely positioned to produce such talent.

How to Involve Students in Purpose and Impact

There are many ways in which universities can empower and enable their students to find purpose and align with and help achieve the university's purpose. Student **volunteering and service-learning**, as in my own opening story, is one such powerful way. Service-learning usually combines an educational experience and learning with volunteering and personal reflection. Students like to volunteer for various reasons, both altruistic and self-centred ones. In a study we conducted with students all around the world (Handy et al., 2010), we found that students volunteered not just for résumé building, but also because they wanted to serve and create impact. People with altruistic motivations volunteered much more than those who only wanted to build their résumés. In another study we conducted on student volunteering in Australia (Haski-Leventhal et al., 2019), we found that a psychological contract existed between the students, the not-for-profit organisation through which they volunteered and their university, which created various expectations in all parties. Successful volunteering experiences met and even exceeded these expectations, but, when student volunteering was not well managed, it ended up in disappointment for the students, sometimes with the university. (For further information on this, there are useful umbrella organisations such as Campus Compact at compact.org providing information and tools.)

One such example is Georgetown University (Urquilla, 2016), which offers a fellowship program, 'GU Impacts', placing undergraduates with innovative public, for-profit or not-for-profit institutions in the USA and around the world. During a 10-week residency, students work with these partners to implement innovations such as educational technology solutions for children in Nicaragua or micro-entrepreneurship development in Peru. When they return, the University helps them reflect on their experiences and draw lessons to inform their academic and career plans.

Another way for students to be involved in the purpose-driven university is through their **student bodies** which are related to purpose. International organisations, such as oikos International, Enactus and Net Impact, are all aimed at offering platforms for collaboration in which students can jointly act and work to create impact. Some of these initiatives are about society, while others are about the environment or both. Enactus (2019) engages over 70,000 students in 36 countries in entrepreneurial leadership to create positive social impact for over 17 million people. For example, they do so by creating innovative ways to heat water in Africa or by developing a mattress recycling facility in the USA (also see Enactus in the Netherlands in Chapter 2).

Students are also involved in their universities' **environmental sustainability**. In Northern Europe and other countries, many students are involved in 'green offices' to lead sustainability in their university. A green office informs, connects and supports students and staff to act on sustainability. It needs to be funded and approved by university management and is jointly led by students and staff. For example, the green office for KU Leuven University in Belgium is the sustainability lab run for and by students. Its mission is to 'make KU Leuven and its population more sustainable, in all its facets' (also see the case study in Chapter 9). Students and staff work together towards this goal through numerous projects, events and campaigns. Students' initiatives to rank universities according to their impact on the environment (e.g. Green League, People and Planet) were also mentioned earlier.

Students are not going to wait for their university to define and act on its purpose. If university leaders will not lead with purpose, students will show them the way with bottom-up student initiatives. However, the support of the university leadership and its stakeholders will yield better results, notwithstanding the power and influence of students.

Graduate Capabilities and Attributes

The word 'educate' literally means 'to lead out'. How are universities helping to lead students out and into the world? One vital way is by not only providing them with a degree but also with graduate attributes which enable them to thrive and create a positive impact on the world.

Graduate attributes are the qualities, skills and understandings a university community agrees its students should develop during their time with the institution. These attributes have become a necessary framework of reference for the 21st century competency-based model of higher education. However, the issue of evaluating and assessing graduate attributes remains unchartered territory (Ipperciel & ElAtia, 2014). Given global uncertainty related to rapid technological developments and the world of work, alongside other equally (if not more) concerning social and political disruptions, the assurance of graduate attributes of employability and citizenship are arguably more critical than ever (Oliver & Jorre de St Jorre, 2018). Graduate attributes include, but go beyond, the disciplinary expertise or technical knowledge that has traditionally formed the core of most university courses. They are qualities that also prepare graduates to be agents of social good in an unknown future (Boud & Solomon, 2006; Bowden, Hart, King, Trigwell, & Watts, 2000).

Traditionally, graduate attributes included cognitive capabilities, such as knowledge, skills, critical thinking and innovation; social capabilities, such as interpersonal relationship, teamwork and communication; and personal capabilities, such as learning abilities and personal growth. These attributes should lead to higher levels of employability, which is an essential outcome for most higher education institutions. Many universities aim to develop their graduate employability because employment rates help them increase their ranking, develop their reputation and serve their students.

Employability is not employment; instead, it refers to a person's ability to be employed. It is the possession by an individual of the qualities and competencies required to meet the changing needs of employers, and thereby help to realise his or her aspirations and potential in work (Yorke & Knight, 2006). Employability enables the individual to move self-sufficiently within the labour market and to realise their potential through sustainable employment. As such, it depends on the individual's knowledge, skills and attitudes, and the way they use those assets and present them to employers (McQuaid & Lindsay, 2005). Many universities also focus on their students' entrepreneurial skills and lifelong learning; with the growing scarcity of jobs, due in part to robotisation, many graduates will need to create jobs instead of finding them and to continuously update their knowledge and skills.

A purpose-driven university, however, also aims to develop additional capabilities in graduates that could assist them not only to study well and find a job but also to create a positive impact and help realise both organisational and societal purposes. These include EQ and empathy; SQ and mindfulness; a global mindset and citizenship; a responsible, ethical and sustainable approach; and a sense of purpose and meaningfulness. Universities may also consider other attributes which might motivate and enable graduates to become an agent of social change who works to create an impact and make a difference.

Academic Staff

There are hundreds of thousands, if not millions, of faculty members in the world today. These employees include full-time and part-time staff, tenured or fixed term. From lecturers to full professors, they are the engine without which no university can run. They are the people conducting the research the university is renowned for and those teaching millennials and Gen Z students. They are often overworked and burned out (Barkhuizen, Rothmann, & Van De Vijver, 2014) because academics must perform complex tasks within an increasingly demanding environment (Houston, Meyer, & Paweai, 2006). However, despite these stresses and strains, many academics are engaged in their work, obtain a significant degree of challenge and intrinsic motivation from their jobs and derive their identity from their work (Barkhuizen et al., 2014). How is this possible?

Academic jobs can meet the three needs or motivators identified by the self-determination theory, or SDT (Ryan & Deci, 2000): autonomy, competence and relatedness. When people meet these needs through their job, they become intrinsically motivated, more satisfied and they perform better, even when overworked.

First, most academics have high levels of **autonomy** and freedom. Based on the principle of academic freedom, most academics choose to work on issues they are passionate about, in both their research and teaching. While there will always be limitations and constraints, which may put pressure on academics to teach courses that are not in their core area of expertise, academics are usually not very remote from this area. The levels of autonomy are even higher when it comes to research and writing articles and books. While most academics are pressured to publish in top-tier journals, they can still choose their field of study and the methods they use.

Second, academic jobs usually offer a high level of **competence**, as they typically require very high skills. One cannot become a full professor without years of education, academic competency development, knowledge and reputation. The learning journey of academics never ends, and self-determined scholars will always be able to continue to learn and develop.

Finally, academic jobs often offer high levels of **relatedness**, which is about feeling connected with others and having meaningful relationships. While there is some level of loneliness working in academia, there are also many opportunities for collaboration. Although one study showed that 40% of academics view isolation at work as the main factor affecting their mental health (Sibai, Ferreira, & Bernardo, 2019), for 60% isolation was not such a contributing issue. Academics often collaborate in the writing of publications, meet at academic conferences and co-operate in their faculties and departments. Universities can do more in meeting this need for relatedness by creating platforms for collaboration. One solution for generating collaboration is through a shared impact purpose, which connects academics to the community and each other.

Pink (2009), the author of *Drive: The Surprising Truth about What Motivates Us*, used SDT and other sources to conclude that what motivates people in the workplace are autonomy (as in the above), mastery (similar to competency) and purpose. Pink defines purpose as the sense that what we do produces something transcendent or serves something meaningful beyond ourselves. It refers to the desire to do something that has meaning, usually with a focus on a 'bigger picture', something more important than just one's own interests. Pink argues that those who believe that they are working towards something more important than themselves are often the most hard-working, productive and engaged employees. Universities still need to provide sufficient financial reward (to 'take the issue of money off the table') but must also enable autonomy, mastery and purpose to motivate academic staff intrinsically.

As such, it is essential to involve academic staff members in developing and achieving the purpose of the university. They can and need to participate in designing, defining and working towards this purpose. Their contribution could lead to new levels of employee engagement and a better defined and achieved purpose (Brooks, Marsh, & Wilcox, 2013).

Schaufeli, Salanova, Gonzalez-Roma, and Bakker (2002) defined engagement as a positive and fulfilling work-related state of mind that is characterised by high levels of energy, involvement and efficacy. Employee engagement is related to dedication to the job, extra-role behaviour and organisational citizenship behaviour (Saks, 2006). However, data show that employee engagement is rather low in the USA, including in higher education, with only 34% of university faculty and staff reporting feeling engaged in their jobs (Gallup, 2017). However, recent data (Gallup, 2019) show a possible rise in employee engagement, possibly due to purpose and CSR.

One example of engaging academic staff and students in impact purpose comes from Bentley University. Located on a campus in New England near Boston, Bentley defines itself as 'a dynamic community of leaders, scholars and creative thinkers' intending to develop students with a 'broad global perspective and the high ethical standards required to make a difference in an ever-changing world'. With a robust service-learning programme for students, academic staff are also encouraged to contribute to these goals. Students and staff work with the university towards its sustainability goals and reducing its carbon emissions: 'Through education and awareness campaigns, students, faculty and staff have become more engaged in Bentley's efforts toward carbon neutrality by 2030.' In one admirable project, faculty and students worked together to teach English to students in Afghanistan over Skype.

Another illustration of employee engagement through purpose is the University of Technology Sydney (UTS), which is also featured in Chapter 6. UTS creates numerous opportunities for academic staff to donate time and money through the University, including to a scholarship fund where UTS matches the donations of staff. UTS also encourages employee initiatives to contribute to its social impact goals. One such initiative that started with academic staff is Ruff Sleepers, a dog-washing service for the pets of homeless people. Each month, they offer a free service to wash and groom dogs, serve free meals and provide a range of donated items, including dog accessories and pet food, to 'those doing it tough'. The team received a commendation in the Elizabeth Hastings Memorial Award for Community Contribution at the 2018 UTS Human Rights Awards for its work on Ruff Sleepers, 'recognising the role that universities can play in having a positive impact on their neighbours and local community'.

Professional Staff

It is beneficial to discuss professional staff separately from academic staff because they often do not receive the same attention and value as academic staff. To clarify, the administrative staff does not refer to academics who undertake a management role, such as heads of department, but to employees who provide administrative support to the university. Professional staff (also named administrative or support staff) are essential to the work of the university. Although academics are those leading research and teaching which are at the core of any higher education institution, the work of professional staff is what makes it all possible. From managing the institution and its facilities to providing bureaucratic support; from fundraising for the university to managing and distributing funds; and from providing teaching and research support to acting as personal assistants, these people are essential to the success of the university.

According to Whitchurch (2008), activity in higher education institutions has been traditionally viewed in binary terms: of an academic domain, and an administrative or management domain that supports it. The 'support' side consisted of professional staff in specialist functions (such as finance, human resources and estates), and in generalist functions (such as student services and secretariat roles), usually in a full-time capacity. However, this division, reflected in terms such as 'academic' and 'non-academic' staff, leads to an 'us' versus 'them' approach. Although the last two decades have witnessed an increase in the blurring boundaries between the two (creating 'para-academic' roles), many universities still hold such a division and hierarchy.

Some scholars (Graham, 2012; Pitman, 2000) have argued that research on higher education is mostly taken by academic staff. Therefore, it has typically concentrated on the contribution of academic staff and largely overlooked the crucial role of professional staff. However, there has been a recent increase in research about professional staff, and sometimes by them. In Australia, for example, professional staff comprise more than half the higher education workforce, and a more rigorous understanding is needed of the contribution that professional staff make to the strategic goals of their institutions.

As explained by Bossu, Brown, and Warren (2018), professional staff are among the university's most valuable assets, as they hold much of the organisational knowledge required to ensure that universities operate efficiently and effectively. Given the contribution professional staff make, and the increasing importance of the roles they perform within their institutions and for society, it is surprising that their work, impact, careers and aspirations remain largely unexplored in the literature and research to date. Professional staff can also participate in defining the purpose of the university and provide time, skills and resources to help it achieve its impact purpose. As such, when discussing the professional and support staff in higher education institutions, it is essential to cover issues of inclusion and engagement.

According to the World Bank (2019), social inclusion is the process of improving the terms on which individuals and groups take part in society, including the ability, opportunity and dignity of people who are often disadvantaged based on their social identity. Being socially included means that people have the resources, opportunities and capabilities to work, learn and participate in society. Workplace inclusion is very similar, except 'society' is replaced by the organisation. In the context of a workplace, inclusion is usually referred to in terms of including women, ethnic minorities, disabled people and LGBTQ+ people. These groups are often socially excluded based on their social identity, or the social groups to which they belong.

Conversely, in the context of higher education, professional staff are often seen as 'second best' citizens due to their role. In general, they are less educated than the academic staff and contribute less directly to the achievement of the organisational goals. A purpose-driven university must be inclusive in the sense that all its employees are given similar opportunities and support, recognition and resources.

As such, the treatment of both academic staff and professional staff is a social responsibility issue. Universities that want to be a responsible employer need to show their social responsibility towards employees first, and this includes both academic and professional staff. Fair management of professional staff, with excellent, stable and safe working conditions is the basis of this. Involving and integrating them in all aspects of university life, including in its purpose, is the next level.

Other Important Stakeholders

While students and staff are the major and internal stakeholders of any university, there are some other prominent groups which can help it achieve its purpose and goals. These external stakeholders include corporate partners, the government, donors (philanthropic partners), the environment and the community.

Corporate Partners

Box 5.1. Oxford University's Knowledge Exchange and Impact Team

This chapter opened with the case of Oxford University to show not only how to create university–industry partnerships but also why we should do so. As Oxford (2019) explains on its website:

> Big challenges face our world today: from pioneering new cures to setting society-shaping policies, from creating new energy sources to determining modern ethics. At Oxford University we're passionate about the creation and impact of our knowledge and how, in partnership, we can apply this to real challenges.
>
> Oxford has unique breadth and depth in its research capabilities, and it is keen to work collaboratively with businesses and other organisations for the benefit of all involved and also wider society. The University actively encourages its academics to take part in collaborations and provides support at all stages of the necessary interactions. Many collaborations are interdisciplinary, or multidisciplinary, and all relationships are bespoke.

To achieve these goals and support these collaborations, Oxford University established a Knowledge Exchange and Impact Team. In addition to research collaboration opportunities, Oxford encourages its partners to build 'strategic alliances'. Oxford University has numerous existing networks which its corporate partners can join, such as the Global Health Bioethics Network, Oxford Business Networks, Oxford Innovation Society, Oxford Networks for the Environment, and the Oxford Network of Peace Studies. It is easy to see how some of these networks can be utilised to achieve impact purpose and help achieve the SDGs.

Universities often partner with other organisations from all three sectors of the economy (business, government and not-for-profits) to achieve mutual goals. Business–university partnerships are valuable, as corporate organisations often have research needs that universities can help address and the resources that universities need. Universities often encourage their staff to collaborate with corporate partners and to bring in financial funds to support these efforts. In Australia, for example, the Australian Research Council (ARC) offers ARC Linkage Project grants where the government matches the financial and in-kind contributions of researchers working with partner organisations. These partnerships can help universities and business to jointly address society's most significant problems, which is the aim of so many universities nowadays. In the Netherlands, the government donated €440,000 to inspire entrepreneurial skills and professional development at the nexus of the private sector, local government and nearby universities.

Rybnicek and Königsgruber (2019) argue that partnerships with industry can help universities achieve their 'third mission'. In addition to research and teaching, many higher education institutions seek to commercialise academic knowledge through continuing education, patenting, technology transfer offices and science parks or incubators. According to this recent article, there are many drivers for such partnerships: companies profit from highly qualified human resources, such as researchers and students; gain access to technology and knowledge; and can use expensive research infrastructure. Universities, on the other hand, benefit from additional funding opportunities, access to industrial equipment and licensing or patenting income. Business can also provide access to data, infrastructure, facilities and work opportunities for students and graduates.

Not every university in the world has the brand, reputation and appeal of Oxford University. Nonetheless, even smaller and less-reputed universities can provide supportive platforms and networks to work effectively with potential and current business partners. However, not enough universities are even exploring the countless pathways for collaboration. In 2013, a national study of institutional collaboration, which surveyed over 400 universities (see Rybnicek & Königsgruber, 2019), found that just over one-half of universities (55%) collaborated with industry in research and development, and only 18% worked with businesses in teacher development. Furthermore, only 16% had a small business incubator. There are unlimited other opportunities for collaboration, including internships, work placements for students, joint innovation districts, scholarships, reciprocal tours and visitations, and guest speaking.

Rybnicek and Königsgruber (2019) offer a model that examines the factors leading to successful university–industry collaboration. These factors include institutional factors (e.g. resources, structure and willingness to change); relationship factors (e.g. communication, trust, culture, expectations and experience); output factors (e.g. objective, knowledge and technology transfers) and framework factors (e.g. environment, contracts and geographical distance). These four groups of factors lead to four outputs: flexibility, honesty, clarity and awareness (respectively), which can lead to positive collaboration results. Fig. 5.2 presents this model.

Purpose-related Stakeholders 81

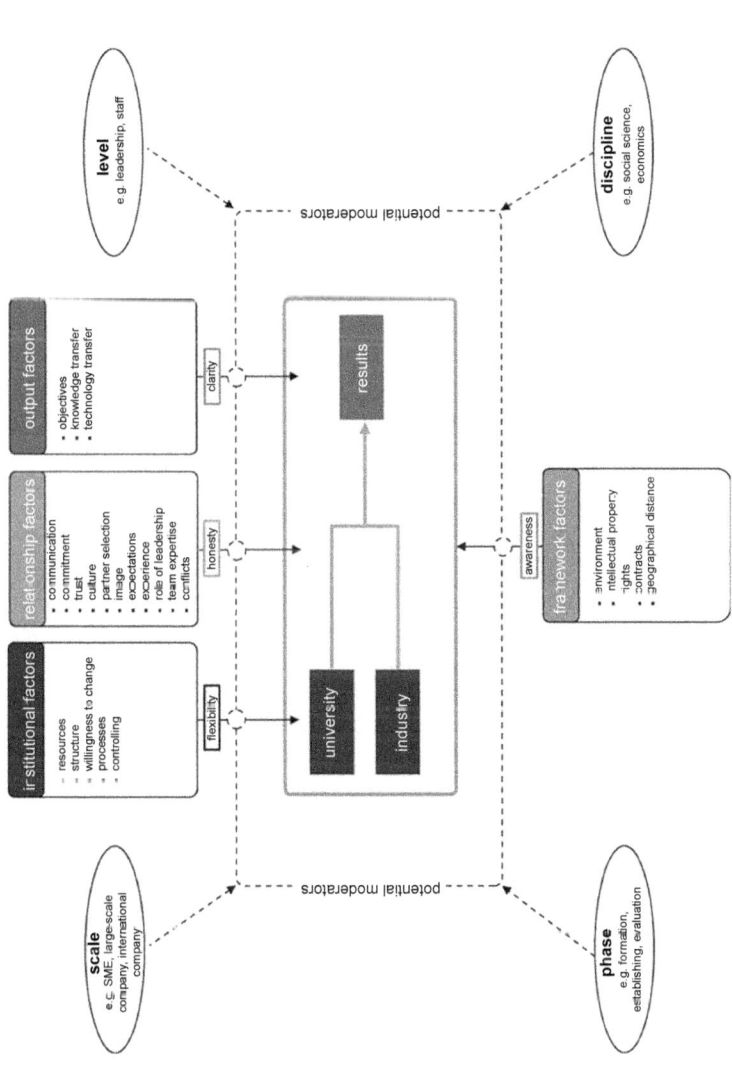

Fig. 5.2. University–Industry Collaboration Model. *Source:* Rybnicek and Königsgruber (2019).

While the model in Fig. 5.2 offers a good contribution to the understanding of success factors in such collaborations, it also misses an essential aspect of any successful relationship and collaboration: shared goals. Organisations do not collaborate unless they can meet their own goals or, better yet, shared goals. A purpose-driven university, particularly one with a clear impact purpose, can create ongoing partnerships with purpose-driven and socially responsible business. With an increasing number of companies emphasising their contribution to society and the environment, having a clear purpose can truly unleash the potential to create successful collaborations with industry.

Government

Governments and universities have had a significant and evolving relationship throughout history. This relationship varies according to regime type, governmental political agenda, values and cultures. In many countries, most universities are public institutions and as such hold a strong relationship with government, mostly with departments of education.

There are countless ways in which universities and governments can support each other. First, numerous universities in the world are the result of some legislation and statute. With many governments around the world aiming to offer higher education to their citizens (free or paid), policy and legislation supported the establishment of higher education institutions, either in general or a specific one. Second, in many countries, universities depend on government funding, particularly when education is free (such as in Germany, Greece, Iceland and Kenya) or subsidised. In addition, there is direct and indirect funding for research, research centres and other endeavours such as business incubators.

Funding and policy can strongly impact the way universities teach and what they teach. A policy change in New Zealand led to broader degrees with a higher return on investment, such as business degrees, and a more recent change led back to support in broader education and research. Consequently, the percentage of people attending university went up from about 30% to over 60%. In the USA, federal and state governments are involved in research funding and student aid. Loss (2014) claimed that only a few students and their families realise it, but the government so heavily supports the higher education sector (in the USA) it would be difficult to operate without it. Examining the relationship between the American government and higher education institutions in the USA in the 20th century, Loss (2014) showed that it moved through several stages: recognising the importance of higher education after World War I; educating citizen-soldiers in World War II; educating global citizens during the Cold War; and moving towards autonomy, rights and privatisation towards the end of the century.

For the government, having a vigorous higher education serves taxpayers (and voters). Higher education creates resilient and educated citizens, with high levels of social mobility and the ability to become productive taxpayers. Universities educate young people and increase their levels of employability, which can help reduce spending on social welfare benefits, where applicable. Universities also provide research which the government can use to increase other desirable outcomes, such as health, science and primary education. Countries with strong higher education institutions usually do better in many other economic and social indicators, and, consequently, China, India and other countries are using higher education to decrease poverty and increase their GDP.

While universities hold their autonomy freedoms (at least in most democracies), they are also accountable to the government due to this legislation and funding. Some must, therefore, hold certain governance bodies and provide annual reports.

Working with the government as a purpose-related stakeholder can serve both parties well. An increasing number of governments around the world have an 'impact agenda' – societal and environmental issues that they would like to resolve – locally, nationally and sometimes globally. Many governments address issues regarding national health, carbon emissions, social inclusion and refugees. Most states are committed to SDGs, the Paris Agreement on climate change action, and United Nations resolutions. Working with a university that is not only committed to educating students and leading groundbreaking research but also to addressing some of these issues and concerns can help the government meet its commitments and better serve society. As such, the government–university relationship is starting to shift rapidly towards issues of purpose and impact. To this end, purpose-driven universities will be better prepared to work with governments in the future.

Philanthropic Partners

Higher education institutions often rely on philanthropy (literally – love of humanity or humankind). Philanthropy is often based on private and organised initiatives for the public good, focusing on the quality of life (McCully, 2008). As such, a compelling and clear impact purpose is vital for attracting and keeping the university's philanthropic partners.

While most universities in the world rely on student fees, governmental funding or both, they are all interested in raising more funds for research, scholarships, infrastructure and other imperative goals. To achieve their fundraising goals, universities work with private donors, corporate foundations, private funds, public funds, alumni, government and anyone who would be willing to pull out the cheque book.

Fundraising appeals are designed to persuade individuals to look beyond narrow self-interest towards the greater social good (Goering, Connor, Nagelhout, & Steinberg, 2011). According to Pérez-Esparrells and Torre (2012), university fundraising is defined as the search for private philanthropic funding by seeking individuals or organisations who share the same goals, values and results of the university. These contributions consist of gifts, grants and cash payments and are often an additional income stream to support various objectives or the institutional development of the university.

A Task Force Report to the Government of the British Ministry of Education in 2004 differentiates five types of gifts: operating funds, annual funds, endowments, facilities support and legacy gifts. Endowments are the most difficult gifts to raise because not only must donors be engaged with the long-term goals of the university, but they must also trust the institution's ability to manage these investments (Pérez-Esparrells & Torre, 2012).

However, the nature of philanthropy is rapidly changing. If past philanthropists were interested in giving large amounts of money to institutions, including universities, nowadays they are looking for long-term partnerships around shared goals, causes and purpose. The fundraising paradigm is changing as more private and organised donors embrace philanthropy as a purpose-filled, values-driven and relationship-based endeavour. In this new paradigm, trustees foster relationships with like-minded people to fulfil a shared purpose and to strengthen a community-benefit organisation with a noble, life-saving mission (Taylor, 2014). Subsequently, purpose-driven universities can attract this new kind of donor.

Developing a purpose-focused relationship with donors is a long-term task. It requires developing a coherent purpose, communicating it with donors, creating indicators for success, measuring impact, communicating the impact back to the donors and continuing the cycle. This work transcends thank-you letters or banquets, and this is what donors are now starting to expect.

Environment and Community

If universities are to develop a holistic approach to their responsibility, sustainability and purpose, the environment and the community should become a significant stakeholder. The ecological environment is becoming such a prominent stakeholder, affecting us and being affected by us, particularly in the era of climate change. While universities usually do not manufacture products and therefore their pollution output is less than other organisations, they still have a carbon footprint which should be minimised. Ways in which universities can cause less harm and make a real contribution to the environment were discussed in Chapter 3.

When a university is driven by an impact purpose to convalesce people's lives, the community also becomes a principal stakeholder. The community can refer to people who live in the same geographical area as the university and its campus(es), as they may be affected by the presence of the university, both positively and negatively. Proactively maintaining a constructive relationship with these stakeholders can help in increasing positive impact and mitigate negative impacts and risks. However, the community does not have to be based on proximity and location. Higher education institutions are also part of a global community, and their contribution to the SDGs can be vital. There is no limit to what a university can do with its local and global community: from student and staff volunteering to innovative solutions to their most critical problems. A purpose-driven university embraces opportunities to work with these prominent stakeholders in order to become more transformational and beneficial.

Imperative Questions to Ask

A purpose-driven university works closely with its stakeholders so that together they may build long-term relationships to enable the achievement of imperative goals and purpose. Purpose, in turn, can also be defined in terms of stakeholder integration and a multi-stakeholder approach. Universities' primary stakeholders are students, academic and professional staff, but their stakeholders also include corporate partners, governments, philanthropic partners, the environment and the community. Together, they make a purpose-driven university and help it create a lasting impact on the world.

(1) *Whom do we impact and how?* Stakeholder integration goes beyond mapping and listing some stakeholder groups. Instead, it is based on an ongoing dialogue with these stakeholders to realise how the university impacts them and what can be done to increase positive, and reduce negative, impacts. Comprehensive research can assist in understanding these stakeholders' narratives and the underlying processes they go through due to their relationship with the university.

(2) *How do we create valid engagement?* Engagement creates enthusiasm, excitement, anticipation and a strong willingness to participate. Universities need to ask what they can do to create engaged students, enthused staff and excited partners. Communicating a strong vision for the future with a clear purpose and impact may be fundamental, but it is not enough. It is also crucial to preserve communication and involvement by continuously sharing a compelling narrative of impact and positive change.

(3) *What innovative platforms can we create for collaboration?* Organisations often avoid working with their stakeholders because this consumes vast amounts of time and energy. But what if there were some innovative solutions to assist the organisation in doing so? Nobody thought that two billion people could connect on one platform until Facebook became a reality. There are innovative solutions out there, from online platforms to large-audience participation (such as the Appreciative Inquiry, which will be discussed in Chapter 7).

References

Barkhuizen, N., Rothmann, S., & Van De Vijver, F. J. (2014). Burnout and work engagement of academics in higher education institutions. Effects of dispositional optimism. *Stress and Health, 30*(4), 322–332.

Bossu, C., Brown, N., & Warren, V. (2018). *Professional and support staff in higher education*. Singapore: Springer.

Boud, D., & Solomon, N. (2006). Work-based learning, graduate attributes and lifelong learning. In P. Hager & S. Holland (Eds.), *Graduate attributes, learning and employability* (pp. 207–220). Dordrecht: Springer.

Bowden, J., Hart, G., King, B., Trigwell, K., & Watts, O. (2000). *Generic capabilities of ATN university graduates*. Canberra, ACT: Australian Government Department of Education, Training and Youth Affairs. Retrieved from www.clt.uts.edu.au/atn.grad.cap.project.index.html

Brooks, D. C., Marsh, L., & Wilcox, K. (2013). *Engaging faculty as catalysts for change: A roadmap for transforming higher education.* Retrieved from www.er.educause.edu/articles/2013/2/engaging-faculty-as-catalysts-for-change-a-roadmap-for-transforming-higher-education

Deloitte. (2018). *Millennial survey.* Retrieved from www.deloitte.com/au/en/pages/about-deloitte/articles/millennial-survey.html

Freeman, R. E. (1984). *Stakeholder management: Framework and philosophy.* Mansfield, MA: Pitman.

Gallup. (2017). *The engaged university.* Retrieved from www.gallup.com/education/194321/higher-education-employee-engagement.aspx

Gallup. (2019). *Employee engagement on the rise in the US.* Retrieved from www.news.gallup.com/poll/241649/employee-engagement-rise.aspx

Goering, E., Connor, U. M., Nagelhout, E., & Steinberg, R. (2011). Persuasion in fundraising letters: An interdisciplinary study. *Nonprofit and Voluntary Sector Quarterly, 40*(2), 228–246.

Graham, C. (2012). Transforming spaces and identities: The contributions of professional staff to learning spaces in higher education. *Journal of Higher Education Policy and Management, 34*(4), 437–452.

Enactus. (2019). *Who we are/our story.* Retrieved from www.enactus.org/who-we-are/our-story/

Handy, F., Cnaan, R. A., Hustinx, L., Kang, C., Brudney, J. L., Haski-Leventhal, D., & Ranade, B. (2010). A cross-cultural examination of student volunteering: Is it all about résumé building? *Nonprofit and Voluntary Sector Quarterly, 39*(3), 498–523.

Haski-Leventhal, D., & Pournader, M. (2017). Business students willing to sacrifice future salary for good corporate social responsibility: Study. *The Conversation.* Retrieved from www.theconversation.com/business-students-willing-to-sacrifice-future-salary-for-good-corporate-social-responsibility-study-73122

Haski-Leventhal, D., Paull, M., Young, S., MacCallum, J., Holmes, K., Omari, M., ... Alony, I. (2019). The multidimensional benefits of university student volunteering: Psychological contract, expectations and outcomes. *Nonprofit and Voluntary Sector Quarterly, 49.* DOI:10.1177/0899764019863108

Houston, D., Meyer, L. H., & Paweai, E. A. (2006). Academic staff workloads and job satisfaction: Expectations and values in academe. *Journal of Higher Education Policy and Management, 28*(1), 17–30.

Ipperciel, D., & ElAtia, S. (2014). Assessing graduate attributes: Building a criteria-based competency model. *International Journal of Higher Education, 3*(3), 27–38.

Leibson, H. (2018). The power of purpose-driven. *Forbes.* Retrieved from www.forbes.com/sites/hayleyleibson/2018/01/25/the-power-of-purpose-driven/#7f0fcc135dca

Loss, C. P. (2014). *Between citizens and the state: The politics of American higher education in the 20th century.* Princeton, NJ: Princeton University Press.

Mackey, J., & Sisodia, R. (2014). *Conscious capitalism.* Boston, MA: Harvard Business Review Press.

McCully, G. (2008). *Philanthropy reconsidered: Private initiatives, public good, quality of life.* Bloomington, IN: AuthorHouse.

McQuaid, R. W., & Lindsay, C. (2005). The concept of employability. *Urban Studies, 42*(2), 197–219.
Odell, P. (2018). *What leaders need to know about hiring the purpose driven generation.* Retrieved from www.chiefmarketer.com/leaders-need-know-hiring-purpose-driven-generation
Oliver, B., & Jorre de St Jorre, T. (2018). Graduate attributes for 2020 and beyond: Recommendations for Australian higher education providers. *Higher Education Research & Development, 37*(4), 821–836.
Oxford. (2018). *Strategic plan 2018–23.* Retrieved from www.ox.ac.uk/about/organisation/strategic-plan-2018-23
Oxford. (2019). *Organisation.* Retrieved from www.ox.ac.uk/about/organisation?wssl=1
Parsell, G., Spalding, R., & Bligh, J. (1998). Shared goals, shared learning: Evaluation of a multi-professional course for undergraduate students. *Medical Education, 32*(3), 304–311.
Pérez-Esparrells, C., & Torre, E. M. (2012). The challenge of fundraising in universities in Europe. *International Journal of Higher Education, 1*(2), 55–66.
Pew Research Centre. (2019). *Millennial life: How young adulthood today compares with prior generations.* Retrieved from www.pewsocialtrends.org/essay/millennial-life-how-young-adulthood-today-compares-with-prior-generations
Pink, D. H. (2009). *Drive: The surprising truth about what motivates us.* New York, NY: Penguin Books.
Pitman, T. (2000). Perceptions of academics and students as customers: A survey of administrative staff in higher education. *Journal of Higher Education Policy and Management, 22*(2), 165–175.
Ryan, R. M., & Deci, E. L. (2000). Self-determination theory and the facilitation of intrinsic motivation, social development, and wellbeing. *American Psychologist, 55*(1), 68–78.
Rybnicek, R., & Königsgruber, R. (2019). What makes industry–university collaboration succeed? A systematic review of the literature. *Journal of Business Economics, 89*(2), 221–250.
Saks, A. M. (2006). Antecedents and consequences of employee engagement. *Journal of Managerial Psychology, 21*(7), 600–619.
Schaufeli, W. B., Salanova, M., Gonzalez-Roma, V., & Bakker, A. B. (2002). The measurement of engagement and burnout: A two sample confirmatory factor analytic approach. *Journal of Happiness Studies, 3*, 71–92.
Sibai, O., Ferreira, M. C., & Bernardo, F. (2019). Overworked and isolated: The rising epidemic of loneliness in academia. *The Conversation.* Retrieved from www.theconversation.com/overworked-and-isolated-the-rising-epidemic-of-loneliness-in-academia-110009
Simms, C., & Chapleo, C. (2010). Stakeholder analysis in higher education: A case study of the University of Portsmouth. *Perspectives: Policy and Practice in Higher Education, 14*(1), 12–20.
Taylor, B. C. (2014). *Purpose-driven philanthropy.* Retrieved from www.accordantphilanthropy.com/wp-content/uploads/2014/07/201407-Trustee-Finance-Feature-Purpose-Driven-Philanthropy.pdf
Urquilla, M. (2016). To build leaders for social impact, universities must adapt. *Stanford Social Innovation Review.* Retrieved from www.ssir.org/articles/entry/to_build_leaders_for_social_impact_universities_must_adapt

Whitchurch, C. (2008). Shifting identities and blurring boundaries: The emergence of third space professionals in UK higher education. *Higher Education Quarterly*, 62(4), 377–396.

World Bank. (2019). *Social inclusion*. Retrieved from www.worldbank.org/en/topic/social-inclusion

Yorke, M., & Knight, P. (2006). *Embedding employability into the curriculum (Vol. 3)*. York: Higher Education Academy.

Chapter 6

Measuring Impact and Storytelling

Sharing Stories of Impact at the University of Technology Sydney

Once upon a time, there was a public university of technology in the beautiful city of Sydney, which decided to promote social justice and achieve social impact as its core activity. It was the University of Technology Sydney (UTS) which embarked on a long and inclusive journey of defining, measuring and sharing its social impact. The University believed that, as public institutions, universities have a critical responsibility to contribute to the community through research, education and practice.

With a total enrolment of over 44,000 students, UTS is one of the largest universities in Australia, defined by its purpose and impact. UTS states that it is measured by the success of its students, staff and partners. It declares itself to be 'committed to research, innovation and the dissemination of knowledge of public value' and that it is, and always will be, an inclusive university (UTS, 2019a). The UTS 2027 strategy, which was developed together with over 4000 stakeholders, outlines its vision to be 'a leading public university of technology, recognised for our global impact' with a defined purpose to 'advance knowledge and learning through research-inspired teaching, research with impact and partnerships with industry, the professions and community' (UTS, 2019b). As such, UTS has three pillars: social justice and accessibility, responsible leadership and excellence in indigenous high education and research.

In an interview with UTS vice chancellor, Professor Attila Brungs, Brungs explained that actions had to proceed the vision and strategy, to avoid 'empty words'. As such, in 2016, the University began developing the UTS Social Impact Framework, through a multi-stakeholder approach. It identified six areas in which UTS must take action, including 'giving students the agency to enact personal and social responsibility'; 'supporting staff to maximise their social impact'; and 'UTS becoming a leading voice in social justice'. The Framework is centred around UTS being an 'agent for social change, transforming communities through research, education and practice'. It has an overarching purpose of 'a healthy, sustainable and socially just society' and three subsequent goals: increased public good, increased social mobility and equity and enabling an environment for communities to thrive. These are immense social goals to aim for, and UTS is expending a vast amount of effort to measure its progress on these goals and share stories of impact.

Working with nearly 150 students and staff to develop the Social Impact Framework, UTS first identified activities around social justice and impact, and collected stories and narratives of change. One of the ways in which impact is measured is through stories of change in the life of beneficiaries. The UTS Social Impact website details dozens of such stories. Each story details the problem, the response, what helped to accomplish this and what was changed as a result. Here is one outstanding example:

> Few of us could imagine being stuck in a foreign country for 26 years without help or support. Yet this is the reality for many refugees around the world, and the number of humanitarian migrants has reached an historic high. A refugee community in West Java, Indonesia, took matters into their own hands to address their access to basic services, establishing their own school. The school has 200 students supported by 17 volunteer staff, along with help from UTS staff.
>
> Refugees who have been resettled to USA, Canada, Australia and New Zealand after attending CRLC have gone into their correct year level at school and make friends due to their English language skills. Their parents report being able to secure employment, feeling confident in negotiating working and living conditions, and feeling better prepared to start their new life.

UTS' commitment to social justice and impact is reflected by a diverse set of institution-wide initiatives that have expanded in scope and depth since UTS was established. UTS declares that its student-based programmes, focused research and innovative teaching practices deliver education and research opportunities to create a more just and equitable world.

One of the leaders of this initiative is The Honourable Verity Firth, former Minister of Education and the current Executive Director of Social Justice at UTS. In my interview with her, she said: 'we live in a world where if you do not disrupt the market, the market will disrupt you'. The Social Impact Framework is a game-changer in higher education, in Australia and worldwide, disrupting the old paradigm of elitist institutions interested mainly in their own success.

Along with other initiatives, UTS helps staff to create impact by providing the UTS Social Impact Grants. These grants aim to support academic and professional staff to maximise their contribution to positive social change, through projects with an 'alignment to strategic areas of impact'. UTS offers 10 grants of up to A$5000 each year for social justice and inclusion.

However, UTS is not only interested in creating and measuring its own impact. Through the Social Impact Measurement Toolbox, the University aims to empower the not-for-profit sector to measure its impact. The Toolbox is a collection of key resources, including online courses with videos, forums, questionnaires, interactive templates and a repository of reliable, verifiable and validated measures, all collated in an open digital platform. Based on a partnership between UTS and Community Sector Banking, the Toolbox was presented in 2018 and the first two courses developed for the Toolbox are now available for free.

UTS works with its internal and external stakeholders to create outstanding social impact and change the world. It enables others to do the same and share a story of its work as an agent of social change and engage many through this narrative.

Introduction

In today's world, in which a record-high number of people attend a university, it is also clear that universities carry a civic responsibility to engage with society and create a positive social impact (Straub, 2019). As with not-for-profit organisations and companies, there is an increasing pressure on universities to demonstrate accountability and responsibility by measuring their impact (Ebrahim & Rangan, 2010). Since universities are public organisations which often rely on some level of public funding, they need to report not only on their success and financial performance but also on the impact they create (Straub, 2019). Gamoran (2018) further argued that the future of higher education is social impact and that universities need to create and measure their value for society.

However, too few universities report on their social impact, and if they do, they tend to report on inputs and outputs, instead of outcomes and impacts. It is, therefore, necessary to discuss what social impact means and how universities can measure it better. It is crucial to deliver not only qualitative results of social impact assessment, such as stories of change, but also quantitative ones.

In addition, universities need to use their impact measurement to share a compelling story of change. Creating a narrative that connects internal and external stakeholders can be a powerful way to create additional impact and receive the support of leadership and others. As storytelling is becoming a more commonly used instrument in marketing, universities must increase their ability to create compelling stories.

As such, this chapter will offer definitions of social impact, explain the importance of measuring it, detail some of the current tools and frameworks to allow more systematic measurement and comparisons and discuss the related challenges and how to overcome them.

Measuring and Sharing the Social Impact

Universities need to share their measurable impact to illustrate how they achieve their purpose. A university is accountable to its stakeholders and to all those who invest time and money in it, working towards a shared purpose. Consequently, measuring the university's social impact is an act of responsibility and transparency, which can lead to higher levels of legitimacy and engagement.

In the context of higher education institutions, Straub (2019) suggested two key measures for universities: the extent to which university projects engage with the public, and how successfully they focus on social challenges in the local area. The author suggests that, in the future, governments may consider providing funding to those universities which perform well on their social impact to enable them to expand this work. As Straub (2019) argued, no matter what exact assessment methodology is used, the first step is to get social impact on the agenda of higher education institutions.

Social impact can be defined as change made to one or more of the following: 'people's way of life, their culture, community, political systems, environment, health and wellbeing, personal property and rights and their fears and aspirations' (Vanclay, 2003, p. 2). Auerswald (2009, p. 52) described social impact as 'the creation of benefits or reductions of costs for society – through efforts to address societal needs and problems – in ways that go beyond the private gains and general benefits of market activity'. Social impact assessment is the processes of analysing, monitoring and managing the intended and unintended social consequences, both positive and negative, of planned interventions (Vanclay, 2003).

While social impact assessment can take time, effort and money, it can also help to improve the way the organisation creates impact. Social impact assessment can provide a constant benchmarking, engage internal and external stakeholders, clarify goals and inspire others to also pursue purpose (Haski-Leventhal, 2018).

Social Impact Tools

There are many social impact assessment tools and frameworks, which differ by their level of sophistication, the knowledge required to use them, target audience and method (quantitative or qualitative). These range from simple tools to use, such as the basic/programme logic model, to the more sophisticated and difficult, such as social return on investment (SROI). This chapter will not cover these tools (for a comprehensive review of these tools and how to use them, see Haski-Leventhal (2018) and other books and articles on measuring impact). Here, we will only illustrate social impact assessment by presenting one tool, the basic logic model, as it is easy to follow, implement and utilise. It may also assist in comprehending the different levels of social impact.

Logic models are frameworks utilised for programme planning, management and evaluation. A logic model (also known as a 'logical framework', 'programme logic', 'programme theory' or 'impact value chain') is an easy-to-follow graphic display of the relationship between the programme's resources (inputs), activities and intended or actual results, both short term (outputs and outcomes) and long term (impact) (Kaplan & Garrett, 2005; Fig. 6.1).

Let us apply the basic logic model to a university sending its students every summer to build houses in rural Kenya. The **input** would include the students and the hours they give, but also the staff working on planning and training the students, and the university's financial funds used to support the students in their journey. It should also include the community resources, locally and in Kenya,

Fig. 6.1. The Basic Logic Model. *Source:* Based on Haski-Leventhal (2018); Kaplan and Garrett (2005).

and materials used to build the houses. The activities would comprise house building, the course the students attend before going, as part of their service-learning, their experience and what they gain from it. **Outputs** are the direct products of this programme. In this case, that would be safe accommodation for people living in rural Kenya. The **outcomes** are changes to the lives and wellbeing of the service recipients and other stakeholders. They include the increased quality of life for the Kenyans who receive the houses and for their families. They also refer to the sense of safety, belonging and pride that comes from owning a house. These, in turn, can increase the physical and mental wellbeing of the recipients. Outcomes are also the results for the students, such as a deep sense of social awareness, meaningfulness and purposefulness. There are outcomes for the university as well, including its reputation as a purpose-driven university, student engagement and graduate attributes (e.g. employability or social and human capital).

The **Impact** is more difficult to assess than the previous four levels. It refers to the macro-level and societal changes over the long term. In the example of students building houses in rural Kenya, the impact could be an increase in safety, quality of life, health and even life expectancy in this country. When the programme is small, it is hard to make such claims. However, if a university sends dozens or hundreds of students every year, building thousands of houses over time, the impact begins to accumulate and grow. In addition, these students are probably not the only ones working to help in rural Kenya, and there is an attribution issue of social impact.

94 The Purpose-Driven University

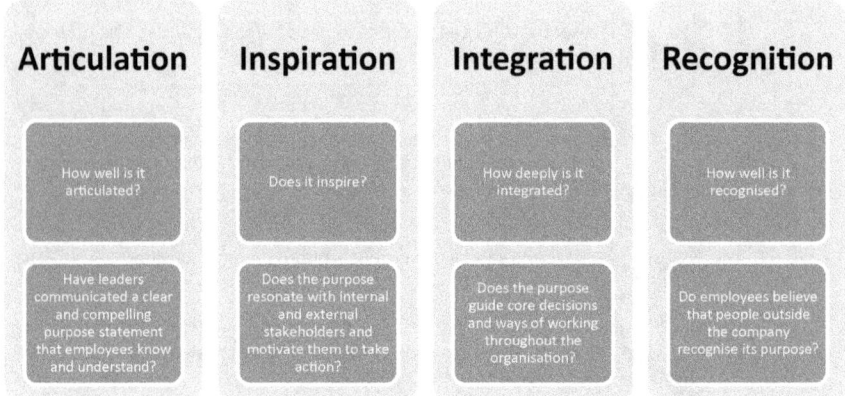

Fig. 6.2. The Purpose Measurement Framework.
Source: Based on Hemerling et al. (2018).

The problem is that most social impact reports, by businesses and by universities, mainly focus on the inputs and the activities. Universities should measure the long-term outcome and impact to assess the effectiveness of their programmes constantly. Measuring impact will not only enable the university to share a compelling story, but it will also lead to an improvement in the work and contribution, higher social return on investment and the best possible outcomes for all.

More specific to purpose, Hemerling, White, Swan, Castellana Kreisman, and Reed (2018) offer a framework on measuring purpose. The framework may assist universities in determining whether their efforts are effective by disaggregating a 'purpose score'. To this end, the authors suggest measuring purpose on four dimensions (Fig. 6.2).

Social Impact Measurement Guide

To measure social impact more effectively, universities need to **start with impact**. According to the theory of change (Connell & Kubisch, 1998), organisations should not start with the input that they have ('students should volunteer, what can they do?') but with the impact they would like to create. Impact creation begins with the identification of a problem in the community, such as poverty in West Philadelphia, that affects that community (and the university) at multiple levels. The university then needs to ask: What could West Philadelphia look like 10 years from today if the university acts? What can the university do to help? What resources are needed to achieve this goal? When the process begins with the impact and moves backwards, it affects the programme and its effectiveness. Starting with the impact ignites debates on the best resource allocation to achieve this impact and the size and shape of these programmes and the university which manages them.

Second, universities need to **set indicators and collect data**. It is essential to develop indicators and measures for the aimed outcomes and impacts in the early stages of the process. There is a vast literature on social indicators, and universities can usually find tools to measure their specific aimed impact. Setting clear and measurable objectives for a programme implies using quantitative measures and a timeline, as well as providing evidence that the impact was achieved. Setting goals, collecting data, measuring timely results and reporting are the essence of social impact assessment.

As a university, there are many researchers who could help in measuring the impact, especially if they can publish the results. In addition to collecting quantitative data, however, it is also vital to collect qualitative data, mainly in the shape of 'stories of change'. To bridge social impact assessment with storytelling, it is crucial to share individual and community stories on how the university worked to shape and change people's lives. These include the lives of the recipients, the students, the community and others involved.

King's College London, for example, is currently conducting a survey of students and the public aimed at identifying its social impact. The survey uses the SDGs as a benchmark. One of the areas where the university is currently achieving the most is in addressing the air quality exposure of children (Straub, 2019).

The next stage of this process is **sharing the data and the stories** with the university's stakeholders and audience. The chapter opening example of UTS, creating a webpage for sharing stories of impact, is one compelling way of doing so. A visual map of impact, such as through the basic logic model, an infographic, images, plots and other tools, can help universities to quickly communicate the impact they have created. Stories should include the impact as well as the outcomes and activities and inspire further action.

Creating a Shared Narrative of Purpose

In 2015, Western Sydney University released its Unlimited campaign. The leading ad featured Deng Thiak Adut, an alumnus, who told his incredible story. At the young age of 6, Deng was taken away from his family in South Sudan, forced to be a child soldier and then shot in the back when he was only 12 while trying to escape. A chance meeting led to Deng reuniting with his brother who helped smuggle him out of the country by hiding him in a corn sack on the back of a truck. The two brothers eventually arrived in Australia as refugees. At the age of 15, Deng taught himself to read, and in 2005 he enrolled in a Bachelor of Laws at Western Sydney University and became the first person in his family to graduate with a degree. Deng now works as a lawyer, determined to ensure that other refugees have the legal advice and support they need before entering the court system. The video of this ad, showcasing Western Sydney University as a purpose-driven organisation, attracted nearly 3 million views on YouTube, becoming the most viewed advertisement by any Australian university and outperforming many leading universities around the world. It is an outstanding storytelling campaign, as it affects people emotionally, and the story stays with them for a long time.

Since the times when hunters and gatherers were sitting around the campfire, humans have been sharing stories, tales, myths and parables that acted as a mechanism to disseminate knowledge by broadcasting social norms to coordinate social behaviour and promote cooperation (Smith et al., 2017). Every culture in the world has stories, as stories are cultural artefacts. Storytelling is universal, occurring spontaneously in childhood, while cross-cultural phylogenetic analyses have shown that folk stories may be highly conserved (Smith et al., 2017). We can relate to the storyline, the characters, their hardships, victories and lessons learned on the journey. A good story can always better illustrate an idea or a moral lesson than just providing facts, numbers or statements. It stays with us. One study shows that, after a presentation, recall for stories was 63% but only 5% for statistics alone (Rush, 2014). There are four characteristics of a good story: (1) goal (why is the story being shared?); (2) attention (why would the audience want to listen?); (3) engage (why would the audience care?); and (4) enable action (why would the audience want to share it?).

As Spears (2017) explained, storytelling is an age-old tool which is precisely what makes it so powerful in achieving organisational goals, such as change:

> A story can go where quantitative analysis fails to gain admission: our hearts and long-term memory. [...] Storytelling uses a communication style that draws on authenticity, personal experience, practical examples and organizational context to provide a narrative that builds support for the change.

Sarah Petherick, senior manager at KPMG International, further explained that good stories motivate everyone to pull in the same direction and to share a bigger purpose. People desire to comprehend and make sense of their roles, and when leaders are good at creating a compelling story, it can motivate employees around a shared purpose (Spears, 2017).

When people listen to a story they enjoy, particularly one that steers their emotions, they activate the limbic system of the brain. Sometimes called the 'emotional brain', the limbic cortex is also responsible for decision-making and motivation. People are emotional and social creatures, and stories tap into this part of being human. Research found that being told a story drastically changes the way the brain works. Functional MRI neuro-imagery shows that when evaluating brands, consumers primarily use emotions (personal feelings and experiences) rather than information (brand attributes, features and facts) (Rush, 2014). When people heard neutral words like 'chair' or 'key', the language-processing parts of the brain (Broca's and Wernicke's areas) were activated. However, when people were told a story, the language-processing areas of the brain were activated along with other sensory areas being used to experience the story.

However, not all stories are born equal; an organisation should aim to seek out a **signature story** that aligns with its strategy and purpose. According to Aaker and Aaker (2016), a signature story is an intriguing, authentic and involving narrative with a strategic message that enables an organisation to grow by clarifying or enhancing its brand, customer relationships and strategy. These authors claim that signature stories represent a critical asset that can be leveraged over time and which can provide inspiration and direction both inside and outside the firm. The challenge is to find, evaluate, gain exposure for and give legs to signature stories.

If a university wants to become more purpose-driven, it needs to start creating and sharing signature stories of impact and purpose. These can be stories about the university's past history, such as that told so well and so vividly by the former president of the University of Texas at Brownsville, Juliet Villarreal García (Chapter 4). They can also be stories of the many ways in which people in the university are continually creating impact and changing other people's lives, as in the example of UTS' work for refugees. Students and staff can become 'stories hunters and gatherers', finding and sharing stories that relate to the purpose and mission of the university. A digital platform where people can share such stories is one beneficial tool to have, and a storytelling team can select the best stories and help to improve them. Another valuable tool is to interview people to record and share their stories. Pictures can also speak loudly, and creating a place for people to share physical or digital images of change can connect purpose to stories.

Creating many purpose-related stories can help to generate a shared narrative of a purpose-driven university. When stories of impact are told well and are listened to by internal and external stakeholders, the entire history and story of the organisation can bond people. A shared narrative creates a collective past, present and future, a sense of direction and an understanding of why it is significant. A shared narrative around purpose and impact can also impart meaning to people's life and work, creating emotional engagement and attachment, a sense of pride, belonging and fulfilment.

Sharing a Story of Purpose: A New Era in Marketing

Today marks a new era in marketing, with purpose-driven marketing. According to Disruptor Daily (2017), the modern world of marketing has progressed through three distinct phases: Marketing 1.0 was product-driven, focusing on the merits of products or services. Marketing 2.0 was customer-driven, focusing on the needs of the company's target market. Marketing 3.0 is purpose-driven. Purpose-driven marketing highlights a company's social purpose and impact, allowing companies to connect and engage with their target audience on the level of their personal values, forming bonds of shared interest and trust that are key to customer loyalty. Indeed, consumers currently want to know what higher purpose a product can serve. Instead of only focusing on the price and quality of a product, consumers are now interested in its 'goodness' – is it good for me? Is it good for the planet? Is it good for society? (Haski-Leventhal, 2018).

This is particularly true for younger generations who are applying to universities. With most of Gen Z (96%) believing companies should help address societal issues, 90% would buy from a company addressing social or environmental issues, and 87% would go online to share a favourable opinion of a company doing good (Cone, 2017). A strong sense of organisational purpose can lead to trust, which, in turn, can lead to working with and buying from this organisation (Hollensbe, Wookey, Hickey, George, & Nichols, 2014).

With the rise of social enterprises around the world, purpose-driven marketing is more prominent than ever before. It refers to the use of a marketing strategy and social marketing to promote purpose, values and mission to benefit others. For example, an Australian social enterprise, Thankyou, uses the power of business to address some of the world's most crucial issues, such as water and food scarcity. Its marketing, including active engagement in social media, is related to its purpose, instead of its products. Purpose-driven marketing is different to CMR, or cause-related marketing, in which a product is marketed with the promise to donate money to charity when consumers buy the product (Varadarajan & Menon, 1988).

Similarly, traditional businesses and universities are now using the power of purpose in their marketing. Airbnb, for example, used its marketing to advocate for social acceptance ('we accept') and LGBTQ+ rights ('until we all belong'). IKEA aired an anti-bullying campaign and Ben & Jerry's connected its products to environmental issues ('if it's melted it's ruined'). These campaigns attract attention, particularly of young people, and are often shared millions of times on social media. As explained by *Forbes* (Craig, 2018):

> Purpose – underutilized in the past – now takes the stage as the heart of marketing and in galvanizing the future of your company. Finding and implementing brand purpose will be central to the growth, innovation and success of all businesses in the years to come. [...] Marketing is more than combinations of images and words to push a product. It's a multi-sensory engagement that promotes greater participation, transformation and evolution, all linked by brand purpose.

Seth Godin is one of the most well-known names in marketing who said that marketing is no longer about the stuff that we sell, but the stories that we tell. Marketing is shifting from selling (products) to telling (good stories). People do not just listen to a good story; they love sharing it and passing it on; and a purpose-driven university can use word of mouth and social media shares to spread its story. In 2013, 34% of consumers used social media to share positive information about companies and issues. However, in 2017, 82% of Gen Z used social media to talk about issues they cared about, and 87% would share their positive opinion about a company that is doing good for the world (Cone, 2017).

TOMS Shoes was established in 2006, with giving as the primary purpose of the company. For every pair of shoes TOMS sells in the developed world, it gives a free pair of shoes to a child in need. Motivated by the poverty he encountered in Argentina, founder Blake Mycoskie has worked to create not only short-term outcomes (giving shoes) but also long-term positive impact. Shoes can provide dignity, a mode of transportation, health and safety. For some children, having shoes implies the ability to walk to school and gain an education, which could lead to social mobility and a decrease in poverty. As of 2018, TOMS has given more than 86 million pairs of new shoes to children in need. In 2015, the company received a brand valuation of $625 million with zero spend on ads – those consumers who love TOMS and its story share it willingly.

Forbes magazine (Craig, 2018) suggested shifting towards purpose-driven marketing by following these steps to engage clients and employees with purpose. They have been reordered and reworded to apply to universities:

- *Create your purpose*: purpose should direct every initiative in the university and impacts students, staff and the community, yet it is one of the most underutilised and least considered aspects of marketing.
- *Innovate and transform*: mission-driven brands possess great advantages, attracting talent and clients. The social purpose must be a directive for the university since sustainability is both a core issue of the organisation and an environmental concern.
- *Embrace growth*: universities should embed purpose so that it shifts from the backburner to direct courses of action. Take measurable and transparent action with authenticity. Let students and staff see how the university evolves in its thinking and contributions and how they can participate.
- *Use active engagement and participation*: students and employees desire to be part of something greater than themselves, and to participate in creating change and cultivating a sense of satisfaction and happiness. It is impossible to do that without a clearly defined purpose. Engage stakeholders in projects and generate innovative ideas.
- *Tell a compelling story of purpose*: if our ancestors told stories around the campfire, the campfire of today is the Internet, YouTube, television and phones. Although people are bombarded with information and marketing messages, a good story stands out.

Addressing Related Issues and Risks

Sharing a story of purpose and impact can be difficult and hold some risks, of which universities should be aware. However, there are also some good tried-and-tested ways to mitigate the risks and address these issues:

- *Honesty and authenticity*. The greatest risk regarding social impact assessment and purpose-related stories is dishonesty and lack of authenticity. If the story is not authentic, or if the organisation is not acting on its stated purpose, it will eventually be called out. Especially today, with the power of social media, dishonesty can go viral very quickly. It is crucial to be authentic and accurate in the stories and data collected and shared. It is essential to have a holistic approach, not using purpose as a one-off marketing campaign, but embedded in everything that the university does.
- *Measuring impact is not an easy task*. It takes time, effort and knowledge to measure impact well, which is probably why so many organisations, even impact-led ones, often report on their inputs and activities instead of on their impact. It is crucial to define social impact in measurable terms, to find social

indicators to measure the impact over time and to use advanced data analysis and storytelling. It is vital to allocate in-house evaluators within the academic staff who can help with this goal. Some accessible tools and indicators can be accessed and used. Not measuring social impact may soon cease to be an option, based on the growing expectation for transparency and accountability in higher education institutions, and it is prudent to be prepared.
- *Inability to embark on community projects.* While an increasing number of higher education institutions are now led with purpose, others are still unsure and reluctant. Many universities are still focused on research and teaching. However, these universities can measure the impact of their teaching and research without leading new work in the community. In addition, universities do not need to embark on new projects. Instead, they can work in partnership with other universities, not-for-profits and additional organisations in the community, to collectively create and measure impact. Impact does not have to be driven by one organisation alone.
- *Purpose marketing can lead to scrutiny.* Speaking to a vice chancellor of a leading university in Australia, he told me that they are reluctant to showcase their purpose and market it: 'if we draw attention to our purpose, people may start scrutinising us more closely'. It is true. Often, companies that claim to be good for the world are looked upon more closely. People come to expect consistency and a holistic approach. However, the solution cannot be to do nothing. Rather, it is crucial to be authentic and holistic, and only to market what the university can wholeheartedly stand behind.
- *We are researchers, not storytellers.* Engaging students and staff, the university's leadership and its stakeholders in storytelling may be more complicated than it seems. Not everyone is a good storyteller, and often such stories may not be told well. However, there will be people in the university with compelling and purpose-related stories to share, and it is essential not to overlook them. It is beneficial to create platforms and recruit talented people who can help to shape these stories to engage both internal and external stakeholders.

Imperative Questions to Ask

(1) *What is our story?* Connecting the past to the present, from the founders to today's students, what is the story of our university? How do we change people's lives? What are the many stories which we can connect into one compelling narrative, connecting all our stakeholders around a shared purpose?
(2) *How can we embed our purpose in our marketing?* Once the purpose is defined, preferably in a multi-stakeholder approach, it will drive the marketing campaign as well. It is essential that the marketing strategy embeds the strategy in planning and executing all communications with target audiences, and that the message is clear.

(3) *How do we measure, share and improve our impact?* As explained in the theory of change, starting with the impact can be an effective way to create it. What kind of impact do we want to create? What will the local and global community look like 10 years from today if we act on our purpose and work with others to achieve it? What outputs and outcomes can indicate that we are on the right track, and how do we measure them? Who in the university has the expertise to help? What activities and inputs do we need to include to achieve this impact? What can we learn from our results to improve the process and the goals? What negative impact are we creating, and how can we address it? What is the best way for us to share our social impact assessment?

(4) *How do we work with others to enable them to create an impact?* The impact of the university does not have to be planned and strategised, nor should it only come from the leadership top down. Students, alumni, staff and partners are continually creating impact in alignment with the university's purpose or on their own. It is essential to involve all stakeholders in the process and to collect their impact so that the university can report on the collective contribution.

References

Aaker, D., & Aaker, J. L. (2016). What are your signature stories? *California Management Review, 58*(3), 49–65.

Auerswald, P. (2009). Creating social value. *Stanford Social Innovation Review, 7*(2), 51–55.

Cone. (2017). *2017 Cone Gen Z CSR study*. Retrieved from www.conecomm.com/2017-cone-gen-z-csr-study-pdf

Connell, J. P., & Kubisch, A. C. (1998). Applying a theory of change approach to the evaluation of comprehensive community initiatives: Progress, prospects, and problems. *New Approaches to Evaluating Community Initiatives, 2*(15–44), 1–16.

Craig, W. (2018). Purpose becomes the heart of marketing. *Forbes*. Retrieved from www.forbes.com/sites/williamcraig/2018/02/13/purpose-becomes-the-heart-of-marketing/#71bfc3c54420

Disruptor Daily. (2017). *What is purpose-driven marketing?* Retrieved from www.disruptordaily.com/purpose-driven-marketing

Ebrahim, A., & Rangan, V. K. (2010). *The limits of nonprofit impact: A contingency framework for measuring social performance*. Working Paper #10-099. Boston, MA: Harvard Business School.

Gamoran, A. (2018). The future of higher education is social impact. *Stanford Social Innovation Review*. Retrieved from www.ssir.org/articles/entry/the_future_of_higher_education_is_social_impact#

Haski-Leventhal, D. (2018). *Strategic corporate social responsibility: Tools and theories for responsible management*. London: SAGE.

Hemerling, J., White, B., Swan, J., Castellana Kreisman, C., & Reed, J. B. (2018). *For corporate purpose to matter, you've got to measure it*. Boston, MA: Boston Consulting Group. Retrieved from www.bcg.com/en-au/publications/2018/corporate-purpose-to-matter-measure-it.aspx

Hollensbe, E., Wookey, C., Hickey, L., George, G., & Nichols, C. V. (2014). Organizations with purpose. *Academy of Management Journal, 57*(5), 1227–1234.

Kaplan, S. A., & Garrett, K. E. (2005). The use of logic models by community-based initiatives. *Evaluation and Program Planning, 28*(2), 167–172.

Rush, B. C. (2014). Science of storytelling: Why and how to use it in your marketing. *The Guardian*. Retrieved from www.theguardian.com/media-network/media-network-blog/2014/aug/28/science-storytelling-digital-marketing

Smith, D., Schlaepfer, P., Major, K., Dyble, M., Page, A. E., Thompson, J., & Ngales, M. (2017). Cooperation and the evolution of hunter-gatherer storytelling. *Nature Communications, 8*(1), 1853.

Spears, M. (2017). *Are you creating a compelling story?* KPMG. Retrieved from www.home.kpmg/xx/en/home/insights/2017/11/are-you-creating-a-compelling-story.html

Straub, V. (2019). Let's judge universities for their social impact, not graduate salaries. *The Guardian*. Retrieved from www.theguardian.com/education/2019/jul/30/lets-judge-universities-for-their-social-impact-not-graduate-salaries

UTS. (2019a). *About UTS*. Retrieved from www.uts.edu.au/about

UTS. (2019b). *UTS 2027 strategy*. Retrieved from www.uts.edu.au/about/uts-2027-strategy/vision

Vanclay, F. (2003). International principles for social impact assessment. *Impact Assessment and Project Appraisal, 21*(1), 5–12.

Varadarajan, P. R., & Menon, A. (1988). Cause-related marketing: A coalignment of marketing strategy and corporate philanthropy. *Journal of Marketing, 52*(3), 58–74.

Chapter 7

Leading the Change

Changing towards Purpose at the University of Auckland

The University of Auckland (2019) was founded in 1883, as part of the University of New Zealand. In those early days, a disused courthouse and jail served as premises for the first 95 students and four teaching staff. Through the first years, most students were enrolled part-time, training as teachers or law clerks, with an increase in commerce students after 1905. It was only after the 1930s that the University became more deeply involved in research.

The 1950s were a difficult period, with student intake soaring after World War II, reaching 4000 by 1959, while buildings were inadequate and overcrowded. In the following two decades, the University of Auckland went through massive building of new campuses, New-Zealand's largest library and the development of many new programmes and courses. In 1962, with the abolition of the University of New Zealand and the University of Auckland Act 1961, the college became an autonomous university. Today, the University of Auckland is the largest university in New Zealand, with 8846 staff and 42,759 students, working and studying on five Auckland campuses, and with 180,000 alumni to date (University of Auckland, 2019a).

The University says its leading position in New Zealand has been achieved by the efforts and excellence of its people, both past and present. However, no university in New Zealand is ranked among the top 50 in the world. Its ongoing challenge is to 'ensure that New Zealand has a major international university that provides a learning environment of the highest quality, leading the advancement of knowledge creation and dissemination, intellectual discovery and innovation, and taking our place on the global stage as a valued peer of the best public civic universities'.

To achieve this goal, in 2012, the University of Auckland embarked on a multi-stakeholder discussion, including with staff, students, alumni and other friends of the University, to develop its strategic plan for 2013–2020. As part of this work, the mission of the University is to integrate academic excellence with a social impact. Its mission was rearticulated, and it is currently to be (University of Auckland, 2019b):

> A research-led, international university, recognised for excellence in teaching, learning, research, creative work, and administration, for the significance of its contributions to the advancement of knowledge and its commitment to serve its local, national and international communities.

Some of its values now include:

- Creating a diverse, collegial scholarly community in which individuals are valued and respected, academic freedom is exercised with intellectual rigour and high ethical standards, and critical enquiry is encouraged.
- Recognising a special relationship with Māori under the Treaty of Waitangi.
- Providing equal opportunities to all who have the potential to succeed in a university of high international standing.

In 2018, the University of Auckland was ranked No. 1 globally in the inaugural University Impact Rankings by Times Higher Education (THE). The new rankings measured how universities worldwide are performing against the United Nations Sustainable Development Goals (SDGs). This outstanding result recognises the University of Auckland's commitment to sustainability and making a positive social impact through its research, teaching and knowledge transfer. In particular, the University came first globally in helping to achieve SDG3 (Good health and wellbeing) and SDG17 (Partnerships for the goals). The University promotes sustainability education in a holistic way, works to achieve gender equality in all academic levels and programmes and has student and staff wellbeing as a top priority. For example, in the Department of Geography, all subjects across the curriculum have an environmental component, and students must think about and explore the meanings of sustainability.

On its website, the University identifies four key elements critical to moving towards sustainability (and purpose): leadership, support, communication and involvement. According to the University of Auckland, all four of these values need to be incorporated into a customised programme that reflects the unique context of the University:

> It is widely recognised that sustainability is a journey, not a destination. A fundamental question, then, is how to keep going when the path is not always clear. The key to answering this question is to recognise that sustainability is an ethical concept, invoking the values that underpin what we care about beyond our own self-interest. To keep going on the journey, we need to internalise the values that underpin sustainability, give people opportunities to reflect on their existing values and practices, test new ways of behaving, and have these confirmed as appropriate.

The University of Auckland did not only shift towards sustainability and responsibility. In becoming more purpose-driven, it also developed a framework for change, with seven stages, which I briefly summarise here:

(1) Assessing the existing organisation and its assets;
(2) Identifying key areas for change and creating programmes and initiatives to address them;
(3) Addressing priority areas of concern while engaging students and staff;
(4) Conducting a baseline assessment before a change to measure effectiveness;
(5) Using baseline data to increase the focus on priority areas and make further improvements;
(6) Measuring outcomes and promoting results to internal and external stakeholders; and
(7) Re-assessing context after each new initiative, finding new ways to show and enable leadership, gain and provide support and communicate effectively.

This framework and the substantial organisational changes that the University of Auckland went through show that becoming a more purpose-driven university can be a long journey, taken by many, but one that begins with a decision and a first step.

Introduction

> The deepest resources for the transformation of business, as for society as a whole, lie within the human heart. It is there we have to seek what it is we truly value and yearn for, and where we can harness the strongest motivation to change – ourselves, our organizations, and our world – for the better. (Cardinal Vincent Nichols, as cited in Hollensbe et al., 2014, p. 1227).

As universities embark on the pathway towards purpose, they lead a profound organisational change. To work according to the suggestions in this book implies an intense transformation, which may comprise the university's vision, mission, strategic planning, stakeholder integration approach, leadership style, impact creation and measurement. Moreover, it needs to include a shift towards a holistic approach of purpose and impact. A purpose-driven university embeds purpose in everything that it does and with everyone it engages, which could infer a long journey towards a new horizon.

The literature on organisational change suggests that this is not an easy task. In his book, *The Heart of Change*, Kotter (2002) argued that most change management processes fail because those people who have to implement the change are not committed to it. For organisational change to be effective, particularly in large organisations, Kotter emphasised that it is not enough to offer people the rationale behind the change; they need to be emotionally engaged in it. Indeed, the most effective way to emotionally engage people in a change process is for them to feel that there is a significant purpose to it; a well-defined 'why', to which they can personally connect. A shift towards a purpose-driven university can offer precisely this. It offers a purpose for the change process as well as a change process towards purposefulness and meaningfulness. People will not change for a new 'what' or 'how', but they will change if they believe in a new 'why'. Any other kind of organisational change will not inspire, engage and recruit people as much as a shift towards becoming a purpose-driven organisation. As such, purpose can become not only the goal for change but also an enabler for any other type of organisational change, providing they are genuinely and integrally connected.

Organisational Change

According to organisational theory and literature, organisational change occurs when an organisation makes a transition from its current state to some desired future state. Organisational change management is the process of 'planning and implementing change in organisations in such a way as to minimise employee resistance and cost to the organisation while simultaneously maximising the effectiveness of the change effort' (Ganta, Chittabbai, & Babu, 2014, p. 10). For this purpose, organisations involve a change management process, which is a structured approach to shifting/transitioning individuals, teams and organisations from a current state to a desired future state (McShane, Olekalns, & Travaglione, 2012).

These commonly used definitions can be easily applied to organisational change towards purpose, by simply defining the future state or desired outcomes in terms of impact and benefiting others. However, for a purpose-driven organisation, a more fundamental and radical transformation is required in this approach. These definitions and many others focus on overcoming the resistance to change and on 'shifting' and 'transitioning' employees as if they were pawns. Conversely, to fully become a purpose-driven organisation with a holistic approach to stakeholder integration, the organisation needs to perceive employees as people who could play a role in this process, respect them and involve them in the process. Most change management processes fail (Kotter, 2002) because they are conducted top-down and outside-in. Stakeholder integration offers a new way of leading a long-lasting and meaningful change.

In Chapter 4, we discussed how a purpose-driven university involves its stakeholders (e.g. students, academic and professional staff and others) in its efforts to become more sustainable, responsible and impactful. We examined the difference between stakeholder management and stakeholder integration, with the latter leading to a genuine conversation and involvement. If universities are to successfully implement change towards becoming purpose-driven, students and staff can be a remarkable source of innovation and positive energy to drive the change, implement it and sustain it for the long term.

In my book on CSR (Haski-Leventhal, 2018), I, therefore, defined change management towards sustainability as an approach to involve various stakeholders in shifting the organisation from its current state to a sustainable and responsible future state. The same approach can be adopted for a purpose-driven university. It is about a stakeholder integration used to help the university shift from a narrow focus on ranking, profits and graduate income towards purpose and societal impact.

To dive more deeply into this process, several organisational change frameworks will be presented to examine how they can be implemented to achieve a strategic and holistic change. It begins with two general approaches to organisational change – appreciative inquiry and Kotter's eight steps, followed by the six insights for change towards sustainability and the eight steps towards a purpose-driven organisation. We will then examine purpose enablers to assist in this process. These frameworks and steps are somewhat modified to apply to the context of this book.

Appreciative Inquiry

When it comes to organisational change, the fundamental approach and assumptions change leaders take can be crucial for the success of the process. A narrow focus on the problem; a failure to provide a strong enough 'why'; a perception of employees and other stakeholders as passive actors who need to be 'shifted' and 'transformed'; and the assumption that change will always lead to resistance – are all some of the common reasons why change processes often do not endure.

In contrast, focusing on the positive opportunity and the new purpose, capturing the strengths and assets of the organisation and its people, involving multiple stakeholders in future design and dreaming about what could be, can offer a completely different approach to organisational change. This different perspective is at the core of appreciative inquiry, an approach to organisational change that is based on positive psychology and focuses on the affirmative aspects of change. Emerging research in positive psychology shows that a focus on the positive rather than the negative aspects of life and work can improve both organisational success and individual wellbeing. It distinguishes itself from other organisational change models by focusing on the best of what is and using it as a platform to build future directions.

Appreciative inquiry (Cooperrider & Srivastva, 1987; Whitney & Cooperrider, 1998) has been gaining interest, legitimacy and applicability. It is seen as a new way forward in organisational change and beyond. Instead of focusing on what is broken in the system, appreciative inquiry concentrates on the positive strengths of organisations (and people) and their possible future. The process involves a search for alignment of strengths, assets and capabilities to utilise them for further success and towards a large-scale change.

It is essential to note that appreciative inquiry is a whole-of-organisation process, not a top-down one. In our case, it requires the university's leadership, faculty, students, professional staff and other stakeholders to actively partake in the inquiry, the design and implementation. Therefore, it is inertly connected to the stakeholder integration approach, aligned with the concept of a purpose-driven organisation and with the ideas shared in this book. Using appreciative inquiry as a strength-based method can help any university recognise what it is already doing in the area of impact and world benefit, and how it can use these 'thousand points of light' to create a shared narrative of purpose.

Appreciative inquiry offers the 'Four Ds Model' (see Fig. 7.1) as the blueprint for the process, and it is possibly the most suitable approach and method for developing a purpose-driven university. The model suggests that as many stakeholders as possible participate in an appreciative inquiry summit where they go through the four stages (or Ds) of appreciative inquiry. In the first state, **Discovery,** they uncover the strengths of the organisation and where its most valuable assets lie. In the context of a purpose-driven university, it could involve the identification of current purpose-related activities, its impact-generating people and assets (e.g. existing networks) that help to connect these people and initiatives. The next stage, **Dream**, is immensely engaging as people start dreaming together about what could be and what is possible. Imagining what the university could become if it were purpose-driven and the possible impacts on the world can be highly appealing. The third stage, **Design**, involves a design thinking method to decide what should be out of all the dreams and visions that emerged in the previous stage. Design involves the process of dialogue, in which participants listen with selfless receptivity to each other's models and assumptions and eventually form a collective model of thinking within the team. Finally, the organisation commits to its new **Destiny** (or purpose) and works to achieve these goals. We can also add a fifth stage, **Delivery**, where the university delivers impact, measures it and shares its story of becoming and being a purpose-driven university.

In addition to the four Ds, the foundation of appreciative inquiry is built on three tenets: appreciation, inquiry and wholeness. **Appreciation** relates to recognising the best in people, organisations and the world. Appreciative inquiry draws on the strengths of individuals and organisations, which then become the foundation on which the future can be built. **Inquiry** is about asking questions and being curious, excited and intrigued. Structured inquiry, such as that enabled through an appreciative inquiry summit and interviews, can help participants learn from one another and together create a vision for the future. Finally,

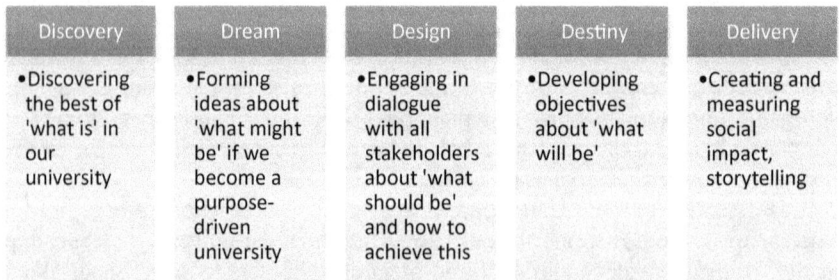

Fig. 7.1. The Four Ds Model of Appreciative Inquiry + Delivery.
Source: Based on Whitney and Cooperrider (1998).

wholeness is about encouraging participation from all levels of the organisation, and even outside the organisation, as the best ideas often emerge from unexpected places. It is a whole-system process.

Appreciative inquiry was used to drive some phenomenal changes. In 1999, using appreciative inquiry and working with David Cooperrider, the Dalai Lama hosted a global religion summit in Jerusalem, Israel, to promote peace between religions. In addition, the Dalai Lama Center has developed the 'Heart–Mind Inquiry', which is designed to engage parents, children and key stakeholders in a change process focusing on the social and emotional learning and development of young people within their families, schools and communities. Furthermore, David Cooperrider was invited to lead the Global Compact Summit in 2004, and the appreciative inquiry was used to engage leaders from all sectors of the economy in reimagining the future of business and the world. Appreciative inquiry was used by Cooperrider to develop the concept of 'business as an agent of world benefit'. This approach focuses on the positive potential of companies to use all their resources to benefit the world. The Fowler Center for Business as an Agent of World Benefit is aimed at advancing the scholarship and practice of flourishing enterprises. It can also be greatly used by universities, not just for organisational change, but also for leadership development, supporting academic staff and realising their purpose. For more information, see Cockell and McArthur-Blair's book (2012), *Appreciative Inquiry in Higher Education*.

Box 7.1. UTS' Social Impact Framework and Appreciative Inquiry

Some universities have been using appreciative inquiry in leading change, including that towards purpose. For example, the University of Technology Sydney (UTS), featured in Chapter 6, used it to develop its social impact framework, to identify what is worthy about the university and what it can become.

For this purpose, UTS organised three appreciative inquiry sessions, where participants were supplied with an interview guide and took turns interviewing each other. The appreciative inquiry facilitator asked participants to share a moment in time where social impact was achieved at its best at UTS. The interview process then guided participants through an inquiry that surfaced the enabling factors supporting the realisation of social impact. The process was concluded with interviewees being asked to imagine a future where social impact was at its best every day. Thinking about this vision, participants articulated their wishes for the future – or what they thought needed to change to enable social impact. In the next stage, data were coded to form the first iteration of the theory of change. A series of workshops with working groups then iterated this work. The emerging framework moved from workshops with working groups to the original cohort who shared their stories, and back until the final version was formulated and affirmed by the community.

Kotter's Eight Steps for Organisational Change

Kotter, a global organisational change expert and leader, offered eight steps towards organisational change that aim to capture people's hearts as well as their minds. For organisational change to succeed, Kotter (2002) suggested beginning with establishing a sense of urgency, followed by forming coalitions, creating a vision, communicating that vision, empowering others, planning for 'quick wins', consolidating improvements and institutionalising the new approach. While some of these steps are imperative, they require modification to become more relevant to the purpose-driven university:

(1) *Embark on the journey towards purpose:* every journey begins with the decision to embark on it and take the first step. It is crucial to get the buy-in from major stakeholders when launching the shift towards purpose, even if the purpose is yet to be defined.
(2) *Form a powerful coalition with stakeholders:* in this step, universities create a coalition through stakeholder integration and work with all internal and external stakeholders to create and achieve a purpose-driven vision. Working with faculty, students, staff, government, partner organisations and donors may lead to assets, strengths, initiatives and impacts that the university leadership alone cannot even begin to imagine.
(3) *Create a vision and define the purpose:* here, the university works with a coalition of stakeholders to define its purpose and vision. Using appreciative inquiry can assist in doing so. The vision is not about being the best in the world, increasing ranking positions and income, but about being the best for the world and how the university can serve others. A well-known phrase from technology says: we always overestimate what we can do in two years and underestimate what we can do in 10. In creating a vision for a purpose-driven university, there is no limit to what can be achieved, and universities can (and should) consider length (of time), depth and breadth, to imagine what is possible.
(4) *Communicate the purpose:* communicating the new purpose and vision needs to be emotionally engaging, using storytelling and metaphors to allow others to see what is possible. Universities need to use every channel and vehicle of communication possible to share their new purpose and vision with all stakeholders.
(5) *Empower others to achieve the purpose:* a purpose-driven university is characterised by shared leadership, where everyone in the organisation gains a sense of ownership over this purpose and a strong commitment to do what it takes to achieve it. This is precisely why it requires a whole-university approach and involvement from the early stages through every step of the way.
(6) *Measure both the short-term and long-term impacts:* according to Kotter, at this stage, organisations need to incentivise and reward employees who are involved in the change. However, based on the approach of this book and in many other scholarly works (e.g. self-determination theory), people are

motivated by purpose more than by rewards (Ryan & Deci, 2000). As such, this step was changed to 'measuring and sharing impacts'. In a study I have conducted on employee volunteering, employees said they would volunteer more if they knew what their impact was. Chapter 6 supports the idea of measuring long-term impacts, and we should still focus on these. However, to resonate with Kotter's notion of 'quick wins', short-term impacts should also be shared with stakeholders to create a commitment to the new purpose.

(7) *Embed the purpose:* Kotter named this stage 'consolidating improvements', where organisations change 'systems, structures and policies' to align with the new vision and hire employees who can implement it. However, here this step was changed to embedding the new purpose in every aspect of the university's life – from teaching and research to service and promotion schemes; from physical campuses and student bodies to new initiatives and programmes; and from who we are and what we do, to who we recruit and what we change.

(8) *Institutionalise the purpose:* this is a crucial stage for leading an organisational change towards the new purpose. No organisation can rest on its laurels after a substantial change process, including a university on its path towards purpose. Purpose and vision need to be continuously measured, communicated and revisited to keep them alive and to ensure that the purpose is not a slogan, but a substantial component of the university.

The Six Insights towards Sustainability (and Purpose)

'The Six Insights' is a paper offering an innovative approach to organisational change towards sustainability. It is based on action research undertaken by the University of New South Wales in Australia in collaboration with other organisations. Hunting and Tilbury (2006) offered a process aimed at helping people and organisations think through the implications, risks and opportunities relating to sustainability. Their insights are also relevant to a purpose-driven university, and this research is an outstanding example of a university working with others to benefit society and the environment. These insights were adapted to align with the context of the book (see Fig. 7.2).

Insight 1: Adopt a clear, shared vision for the future. Here, 'vision' can be replaced with 'purpose' or both can be included. What is imperative is that this vision and purpose are well defined and shared by everyone, so that a sense of ownership and affiliation is created.

Insight 2: Build teams, not just champions. Change agents and champions can help lead organisational change. However, a team-based approach is vital to get a whole-university commitment to the new purpose. Teamwork can lead to innovation, creativity, organisational imagination and courage – all required for a purpose-driven university.

Insight 3: Use critical thinking and reflection. Critical thinking is crucial in identifying the various elements of a change situation (including power structures and personal biases) and reflecting on why things work or not. This reflection is

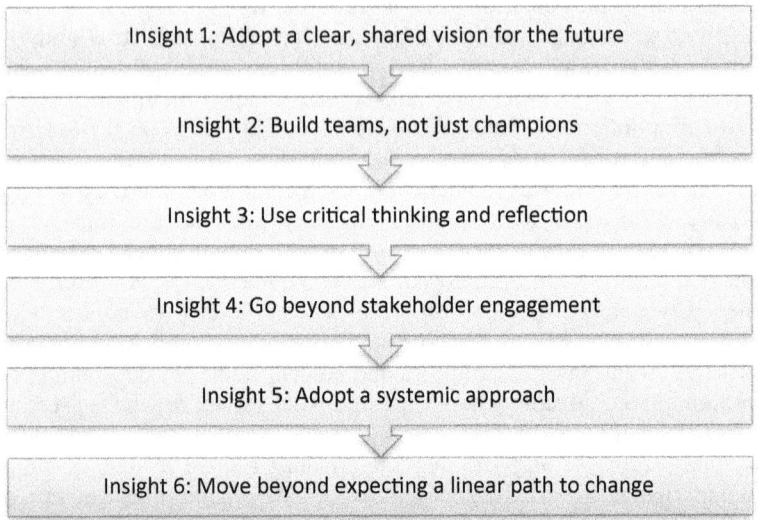

Fig. 7.2. Six Insights Towards Sustainability. *Source*: Based on Hunting and Tilbury (2006).

then used to build a pathway to purpose. Critical thinking and reflection can help a university to comprehend the effect that these levers (including leadership, power structures, politics, hierarchy, collaboration systems and networks) have on its ability to become more purpose-driven, and what needs to change in order to achieve the new purpose.

Insight 4: Go beyond stakeholder engagement. While it is essential to work with a broad set of stakeholders, the university needs to ask why it engages with stakeholders. Is it to minimise risk or is it due to a genuine interest in the input of others, so the university can collectively make changes towards sustainability? To become more purpose-driven, universities need to work more proactively with a variety of other organisations (including other universities) and share information, issues and practices until a 'tipping point' for a purpose is reached. This requires rethinking the traditional stakeholder engagement approach and building cross-sectorial partnerships.

Insight 5: Adopt a systemic approach. Systems thinking looks at the whole (the 'bigger picture'), accepts uncertainty and ambiguity, expands our worldview, recognises that there are many ways of learning and encourages more participatory and holistic approaches to identifying better sustainability strategies. A purpose-driven university requires not only a 'whole-of-the-institution' approach but also an 'outside-the-institution' approach, which implies continually working with external stakeholders in partnerships for purpose.

Insight 6: Move beyond expecting a linear path to change. Universities need to realise that the process of change towards purpose needs to be more iterative and reflective, addressing issues as they occur and often taking a branch path. It is not a linear shift from point A to point B, but rather a flexible and potentially more opportunistic process. Adopting such an approach and being open-minded can also result in innovative, productive and unexpected outcomes.

Eight Steps for Creating a Purpose-Driven Organisation

This next framework was published by *Harvard Business Review* (Quinn & Thakor, 2018). Through consulting work with hundreds of organisations, research and interviews with dozens of leaders, Quinn and Thakor offered eight steps towards a purpose-driven organisation. They have come to see that 'when an authentic purpose permeates business strategy and decision making, the personal good and the collective good become one' (p. 81). These steps (with some modification) are:

(1) *Envision an inspired workforce.* This step begins with imagining what the organisation could become when a higher purpose inspires employees and other stakeholders. A higher purpose could facilitate employee engagement and a workforce that is inspired and aspires for more.
(2) *Discover a higher purpose.* According to the authors of this article, a higher purpose cannot be invented; it already exists. It can be discovered through empathy – by feeling and understanding the deepest common needs of the workforce. To achieve this requires asking provocative questions, listening and reflecting.
(3) *Recognise the need for authenticity.* A higher purpose cannot be 'forged' to gain related benefits or to address external pressures. Purpose must be authentic, and until the organisation can truly stand behind its purpose, it is best not to promote it as a purpose-driven one. As the authors of the article say, 'if your purpose is authentic, people know because it drives every decision, and you do things other organisations would not'.
(4) *Turn the authentic message into a constant message.* This too echoes the ideas presented in this book. Discovering the purpose is not a task to accomplish and finish. Envisioning the purpose of the university, communicating it, creating full ownership and commitment to it and revisiting it require constant work. However, when the message is coherent, it penetrates the collective consciousness, culture and people.
(5) *Stimulate individual learning.* When the organisation becomes more purpose-driven, so do the people it employs. A university can become a destination of choice for people who are intrinsically motivated by a sense of purposefulness and meaningfulness. Such people are also motivated to learn new skills and ideas to achieve their own purpose and the organisational purpose. A purpose-driven university can offer this so that the workforce becomes more adaptive and innovative. Particularly for academic staff and students, who are already on the learning journey, this could resonate and be highly motivating. Purpose-driven universities do not just educate students and provide them with a degree; they offer students the opportunity to live a purposeful life.

(6) *Turn mid-level managers into purpose-driven leaders.* In the context of higher education institutions, these would be academic staff, professional managers, leaders of student bodies and others who are capable and willing to share purpose leadership.
(7) *Connect the people to the purpose.* A genuine connection to the purpose requires the involvement of people in the process. Staff and students need to help steer this process because purpose is then more likely to permeate the culture and shape the way people think, feel and behave.
(8) *Unleash the positive energisers.* Every organisation has change agents or a 'network of positive energisers'. These are mature, purpose-driven people with an optimistic orientation, who naturally inspire others. They are open and willing to take the initiative. Once enlisted, they can assist with every step of the journey towards a purpose. These people can help with each of the previous seven steps.

Box 7.2. The University of Michigan's Strengths for Social Good

Quinn and Thakor (2018) bring the example of the University of Michigan, where Deborah Ball, a former dean of the School of Education, sought to clarify her organisation's purpose to increase employee commitment and collaboration. To do so, she interviewed every faculty member to find a surprising commonality, an emerging story about the faculty's strong desire to have a positive impact on society. Ball captured what she heard and shared it with the people she interviewed, to further capture reactions and refine the shared narrative. Ball said: 'You identify gold nuggets, work with them, clarify them, integrate them, and continually feed them back'. In doing so, it became clear to Ball and others that the school had strengths it could use for social good. For example, it had the capacity to influence how other institutions around the world trained teachers, addressed issues of educational affordability and served underrepresented populations. Ball concluded that these foci had the greatest potential to integrate faculty members' efforts, draw impressive new hires and attract funding for research. She highlighted them as crucial elements of the school's collective identity and new purpose.

Purpose Enablers

It is crucial to identify enablers which can help elevate the change process towards becoming a purpose-driven university.

First, as a common thread through this book, are the **people** without whom there is no university. Enthused staff, students and partners can enable a long-term and profound change in the university. When they share the same cause, people become the strongest advocates for the change and also encourage others to support it. Impact purpose is about societal impact and serving the community. Such people are those who could lead and implement the impact initiative through volunteering, working sustainably and participating in social activism.

The power of people as enablers of change can never be underestimated; they are crucial. A purpose-driven university attracts purpose-driven people, and purpose-driven people make a purpose-driven university.

Second, the **leadership** of the university, from presidents and vice chancellors to deans, heads of departments and other mid-level managers, is an enabler of the change. It is not impossible for a university to become purpose-driven without the support of the person at the top, but it does make it more difficult and less convincing. At the very least, university leaders need not be an obstacle for the change, should it occur as a bottom-up movement. Preferably, they should support it, champion it and lead it.

A third enabler is the **history, story and culture** of the organisation. In many of the purpose-driven universities featured in this book, the history was significant. Even if the university shifted away from its initial purpose, the founders may have built a university to create impact and serve others. For example, Stanford University was founded in 1885 by senator Leland Stanford 'to promote the public welfare by exercising an influence on behalf of humanity and civilization'. Drexel University was founded in 1891 to 'provide educational opportunities in the practical arts and sciences for women and men of all backgrounds'. These original ideas and purposes can provide a historical and valid justification for an organisational change towards purpose. In addition, the cultural strengths of the institution are essential. Every organisational culture probably has some negative aspects, but people more often ignore the positive ones which can enable a long-lasting change (Katzenbach & Harshak, 2011). Such cultural strengths include collegiality, innovation and respect. Alignment between cultural strengths and organisational values can become a strong enabler. Finally, inspirational stories which connect people to the new purpose and to each other (see Chapter 6) are an enabler. They support the organisational and cultural change and make the new purpose more accessible and memorable.

Finally, taking **a holistic approach** towards purpose and the organisational change is a vital enabler. A holistic approach requires a robust motivation to become a purpose-driven university and embedding the purpose in every aspect of the university's life, actions and identity. Consistency is an enabler as it helps existing and new staff and stakeholders make sense of the new culture. Furthermore, if everyone is involved and everything is aligned, interconnectedness and interdependency are created in which people, stories, purpose and all other aspects are woven together to create a new kind of organisation.

Imperative Questions to Ask

There are five imperative questions that any university needs to ask itself prior to undertaking the journey towards purpose. These questions can be raised and answered by all stakeholders of the university, not just its formal leadership. They focus on the essence of change, its direction and the manner required to achieve it. They present the where, why, what, who and how of organisational change towards purpose:

(1) **Where** *do we want to be?* The question of 'where' is about the vision of the university, not just for itself, but also for society. What if we could make a difference in the world? What could the university become in 10 years' time if we embed purpose today? What will be the impact on the world?
(2) **Why** *do we need to change?* Starting with the 'why' is always beneficial but particularly so in changing towards purpose. If the university does not have a strong enough 'why' that resonates with students and staff, the employees might resist the change. The shift towards a purpose-driven university provides its own internal 'why', but it still needs to be discovered and communicated well.
(3) **What** *needs to change?* The questions of the 'what' are particularly significant if the university is to adopt a holistic approach towards purpose. Universities which undergo a holistic change towards purpose need to examine their strategic planning, mission, vision, values, culture, leadership, workforce, practices and policies. In a higher education context, what also needs to change is the curriculum and the research or, more specifically, their purpose and the way their impact is measured. Consequently, universities may need to embrace new ways of conducting performance appraisal, promotion processes and student admission.
(4) **Who** *will be part of the change?* A purpose-driven university is based on stakeholder integration and, consequently, everyone whose life is touched by the university could potentially be (and perhaps should be) part of this journey. Academic and professional staff can lead purpose-related initiatives and participate in the effort. Students can be involved and informed on the changes and encouraged to lead their own bodies, movements and activism. Donors can align with the university's purpose and help achieve it. Partner organisations from all sectors can collaborate around a shared purpose. The organisational change towards a purpose-driven university cannot be led by the executive group alone; it really does require a whole village.
(5) **How** *will we achieve our purpose?* Becoming a purpose-driven university requires a blueprint, a map or a designed plan. Based on the ideas from transformational leadership (see Chapter 4), universities need to develop a vision/purpose, communicate it, model it and create the shared commitment of all stakeholders. Using the frameworks presented here can assist in guiding the university towards this goal.

References

Cockell, J., & McArthur-Blair, J. (2012). *Appreciative inquiry in higher education: A transformative force.* San Francisco, CA: John Wiley & Sons.

Cooperrider, D. L., & Srivastva, S. (1987). Appreciative inquiry in organizational life. *Research in Organizational Change and Development, 1,* 129–169.

Ganta, C. V., Chittabbai, V., & Babu, K. N. (2014). Managing organizational change. *International Journal of Combined Research & Development, 2*(2), 9–17.

Haski-Leventhal, D. (2018). *Strategic corporate social responsibility: Tools and theories for responsible management.* London: SAGE.

Hunting, S. A., & Tilbury, D. (2006). *Shifting towards sustainability: Six insights into successful organisational change for sustainability*. Sydney, NSW: ARIES.

Katzenbach, J., & Harshak, A. (2011). Stop blaming your culture. *Strategy+Business*, 62, 35–42.

Kotter, J. P. (2002). *The heart of change: Real-life stories of how people change their organizations*. Boston, MA: Harvard Business Press.

McShane, S., Olekalns, M., & Travaglione, T. (2012). *Organisational behaviour: Emerging knowledge, global insights*. Sydney, NSW: McGraw-Hill.

Quinn, R. E., & Thakor, A. V. (2018). Creating a purpose-driven organization. *Harvard Business Review*, 96(4), 78–85.

Ryan, R. M., & Deci, E. L. (2000). Self-determination theory and the facilitation of intrinsic motivation, social development, and wellbeing. *American Psychologist*, 55(1), 68–78.

University of Auckland. (2019a). *University history*. Retrieved from www.auckland.ac.nz/en/about-us/about-the-university/the-university/university-history.html

University of Auckland. (2019b). *The university*. Retrieved from www.auckland.ac.nz/en/about-us/about-the-university/the-university.html

Whitney, D., & Cooperrider, D. L. (1998). The appreciative inquiry summit: Overview and applications. *Employment Relations Today*, 25(2), 17–28.

Chapter 8

The Purpose-Driven University Model: Six Steps for Holistic Implementation

Introduction

This book is aimed at helping universities to holistically become more purpose-driven in order to create a stronger impact and benefit society. To achieve this goal, the book has presented numerous concepts and ideas that may assist universities in becoming more purpose-driven. We commenced this journey by examining what purpose is and what the difference is between purpose and related concepts such as mission, vision and values. We then discussed the prominence and benefits of having a clear impact purpose for any organisation but also universities. This was followed by a comprehensive implementation of ideas, concepts and frameworks from the fields of CSR, ethics, sustainability and conscious capitalism, to offer a holistic approach to responsible and sustainable universities. Next, the book shed light on the significance of university leadership in the journey towards purpose, and the most suitable leadership styles in this context, such as purpose-driven leadership, transformational leadership, servant leadership and conscious leadership, with an emphasis on informal leadership as a common thread. The stakeholder theory was used to discuss the primary stakeholders of any higher education institution and how universities can improve their stakeholder integration. As a purpose-driven university is about creating a positive impact in the world, the following chapter discussed social impact measurement and sharing a strong narrative of change. Finally, the previous chapter focused on leading organisational change in universities, using several general frameworks on change and frameworks on changing towards sustainability and purpose. However, no framework exists on organisational change for those universities who desire to become more purpose-driven, and therefore this chapter will offer one.

This framework, the Purpose-Driven University Model, is based on all aspects discussed in this book to offer a step-by-step blueprint for holistic implementation. In a way, it is a good summary of the book but also a toolbox. As such, some parts of this framework will look familiar, while others will offer new ideas.

It is essential to note that organisational change is not always linear or even circular. While the model in Fig. 8.1 looks structured and well organised, it will

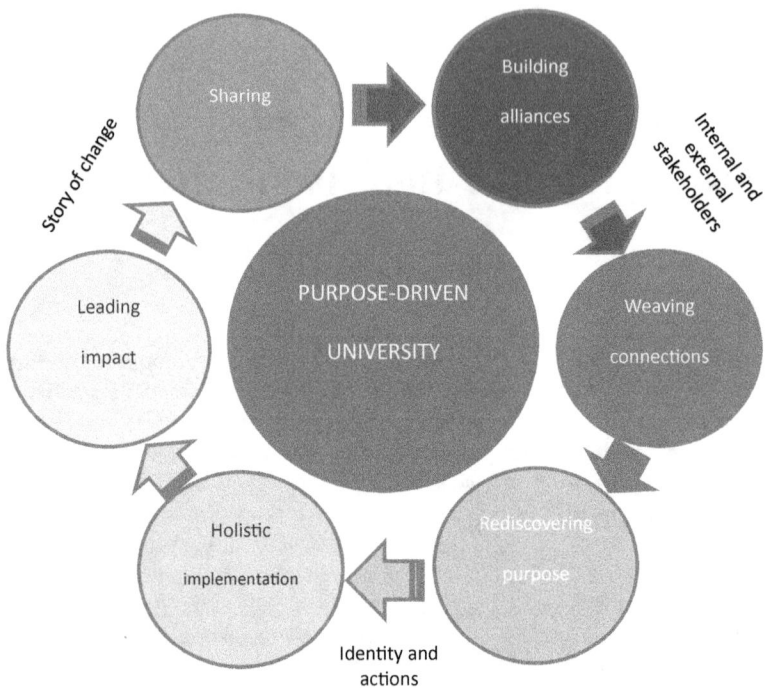

Fig. 8.1. The Purpose-Driven University Model.

not always work accordingly. With numerous variables, such as the university's culture, people, leadership, history, related experiences and environment, no two universities will undergo the exact same journey. Some universities may need to start from Step 3 and move back to Step 1 or move back and forth between the first three stages before they are ready to move to Step 4. However, it is crucial to be aware of these critical steps and not skip them for convenience, lack of resources and a desire to finish the process quickly. Each step is critical in the success of the purpose-driven university, and there are innovative ways to work beyond the resources currently held to include them all. Many people in the university would be enthusiastic about this journey and would be happy to take part in it. Working with the university's academic staff to help collect the required data or measure impact is just one such innovative way.

The central message to convey before presenting the Purpose-Driven University Model is that it should not be implemented top-down. Doing so will be less optimal and perhaps counterproductive. It contradicts the essence of the purpose-driven university idea and definition, which are based on stakeholder theory and a whole-organisation and outside-the-organisation approach. The university leadership's active and vocal support is imperative, but it cannot be their initiative and implementation alone.

The Purpose-Driven University Model has six steps. It begins with building alliances and weaving connections – both oriented towards internal and external stakeholders. These are both about exiting the boardroom to capture existing impact-creating initiatives and purpose-related stakeholders to help the university evolve. The next two steps, rediscovering purpose and holistic implementation, refer to building the identity of the university as purpose-driven and acting upon it. As such, these two steps relate to identity and action. Finally, leading impact and sharing are related to the story of change – how the university is changing, how it further creates change and how it shares it with the world.

Building Alliances

It may seem logical that the first step towards a purpose-driven university would be to define the purpose of the organisation. Nonetheless, as it requires a whole-university and outside-the-university approach, the first step is *building alliances*. Initially, it was supposed to be 'stakeholder mapping' to identify all the impact-related projects and stakeholders. Building alliances is stronger than this.

Building alliances is not a mere action but a mindset. It means that the organisation and its leadership accept that if the goal is to become more purposeful, they need to have the moral courage and open-mindedness to work with others, who may have different experiences, approaches and perspectives. It would be easier to hire a consultancy firm and pay it a vast amount of money to deliver a shiny report with a purpose statement and the marketing strategy aligned with it. On the one hand, creating long-lasting relationships with internal and external stakeholders requires emotional labour, genuine effort and even vulnerability. Nonetheless, not doing so will prevent the university from yielding the full benefits of a purpose-driven organisation. Becoming a purpose-driven organisation is not an end result, it is a process, and the process is just as significant. As portrayed in other chapters, it requires a whole village to create impact and live by an impact purpose.

Building alliances around purpose implies that every person and organisation interested in promoting the purpose and who can contribute to it deserves a seat at the table. It may require a mapping exercise to understand the complex human system to which the university belongs. It is essential to identify and summon all interested parties to take part in this process while being sensitive to diversity and ensuring everyone is included, even if their current voice is not as strong as others'. This implies proactively involving women, people from different ethnic backgrounds, people who cope with disabilities, and others in the conversation. The university needs to ensure that students and professional staff are represented, as well as others in the community.

Building alliances is based on the ideas discussed in Chapter 5, including stakeholder integration and working with the purpose-related stakeholders. Trying to lead the change towards purpose in my own university, people were excited by the idea and expressed a strong desire to partake in this work. Stakeholder mapping can be done using tools such as social network mapping but also by using word of mouth and asking people who are keen to find and invite others to work on this. Building alliances takes time, and it cannot be done too quickly just to tick the 'stakeholder collaboration' box. I have been involved in academic and other collaborations which were built on a list made up hastily by one person and where many other people who would have liked to participate and could make a substantial contribution were left out.

Building alliances will not only lead to higher levels of engagement and lower levels of resentment and resistance, it will also enable change-leaders to realise existing assets in the form of purpose-driven and impact-creating people, initiatives, projects, programmes and ideas. Universities are already creating purpose, and it is essential to capture it, focus on it, frame the university's mission around it and enable further such work. Internal staff can map these initiatives and discuss others with those stakeholders identified at this stage. It is beneficial to create a website, similar to the one used by the University of Technology Sydney (see the opening case in Chapter 6), in which people upload projects, ideas and stories of impact. Such a platform then becomes a virtual campfire for the tribe to share stories around, and an engaging way to identify existing work.

> A purpose-driven university builds alliances, which involves a change in mindset, identifying internal and external purpose-related stakeholders, inviting interested people and organisations to partake in this process, and a mapping of relevant stakeholders and purpose-driven initiatives.

Weaving Connections

> Weaving is a way of life and a state of mind, not a set of actions. It's about the spirit of caring you bring to each interaction with someone else. It's a willingness to be open and loving, whether you get anything in return. As humans, we long for honest, deep connection. Weavers make the effort to build those connections and make others feel valued. (The Aspen Institute, 2019)

The second stage takes place after an initial identification of purpose-related stakeholders and initiatives. When there are enough interested allies, it is time to start weaving connections and bringing down silos.

Many purpose-driven people often work in silos. There may be 'one thousand points of light' working in the organisation, but if they are not connected, their light will not shine through as strongly as it could. By bringing down silos in the organisation, people get acquainted with each other's work, find inspiration in it, teach and share learnings with each other and create additional opportunities and initiatives for impact, in order to strengthen and integrate the organisation.

Weaving connections within the university means a constant encouragement to shift away from **a competitive model to a collaborative one**. This can be challenging, with many academics who are high achievers and sometimes highly competitive and with years of encouraging silos. If, for example, a university recognises sole authorship of articles as more highly regarded than co-authorship, it is encouraging silos. If people are only promoted based on their publications and not on their service, it is encouraging silos. If academic staff are not connected to professional staff, it is encouraging silos. Moreover, if research and teaching are not connected to impact and the community, it is encouraging silos. Quest University in Canada, which will be mentioned in the next chapter, brought down silos by having no departments and no faculties, setting people from different disciplines in neighbouring offices. The result was a high level of collaboration and innovative ideas such as the mathematics of music.

A purpose-driven university weaves connections. This powerful term resembles the idea of weaving threads to make a stronger fabric. Weaving connections throughout the university and between the university and other organisations, will make the social fabric of the university more enduring and enable the possibility of real and powerful societal impact. Universities that improve their capacity to weave connections do nothing less than build resilient communities and social capital. Weaving creates relationships, trust and the ability to see and help others who may be falling outside the current social fabric.

To weave connections, the university needs to create an organisational culture and climate that encourage co-work and collaboration, and opportunities for people to meet and talk to each other. This can be done face to face or virtually, but it needs to be often enough that relationships remain strong. At this stage too, it is possible to find those internal stakeholders who may help in achieving this goal, or the 'weavers'. According to Aspen Institute (2019), weavers work to create a better future, a nation or an organisation brimming with deep and healthy connections, where mutual trust and connections are the standards, equality is implicit and all people find joy and meaning in their life and work. As such, it is clear that the concept of weaving connections is strongly related to purpose and should be a vital step in the journey towards a purpose-driven university.

> A purpose-driven university, therefore, connects stakeholders, people, organisations and initiatives to create relationships, collaborate, rediscover its purpose and create a positive impact in and with the community.

Rediscovering Purpose

Initially, this stage was named 'defining purpose'. It seemed natural that once all stakeholders are aligned, the current purpose-related initiatives are identified, and they are all interconnected, there emerges a community to initiate the university's journey towards purpose. The next stage would be to define the impact purpose in terms of the ways in which the university might utilise its resources, power, people, talent, intellect and even the physical campuses to create impact. However, I eventually decided to call it 'rediscovering purpose' because, in a way, the purpose already exists. It only requires to be unveiled.

To define its impact purpose, a university needs to rediscover who it is as a university – what sets it apart from the other 10,000 universities in the world? What are its unique assets and strengths? What is the unique value proposition of the university? The university value proposition could be, for example, exceptional research or a strong relationship with industry. It may be its successful alumni or its glorious history. However, revolving the value proposition around the unique purpose impact can be a more effective and engaging way of achieving it.

Unfortunately, however, not every university can communicate well what it stands for. As one provost I interviewed candidly said: 'I know what Harvard University stands for and I know what Stanford University stands for, but I do not know what our university stands for.' If the executive leadership does not know what the university stands for (or if only they know it, but the students and staff do not), it is time to consider the positioning of the university's brand in the market. Doing so around impact purpose can be an inspirational way to define and position a university.

As such, this step involves rediscovering impact. It requires a conversation on the impact that has already been created within a university. This impact could be created through core activities such as research, for example, and this can be captured by asking scholars to demonstrate how they create impact through their research. Academics often report on their research impact in terms of the citations and impact factors of the journals they publish in, not on community impact. Social impact can also be created through other initiatives, such as service-learning and students' social activism. There is also a relational impact created for the university's partners, such as community and business partners.

Only after the university rediscovers what it stands for and what impact it creates, can it rediscover its purpose. To do so, it needs to **connect strengths and impact** to make a long-lasting contribution which defines it as an organisation and enables the university to maximise its contribution to the world. This is impact purpose, which is strongly and strategically aligned with the brand of the university and what it stands for.

Rediscovering purpose can present an excellent opportunity not only to offer a well-defined purpose statement, based on stakeholder consultation, but also to re-examine the university's vision, mission and values. While these three should not change too often, and some universities do not change them at all, if there is an opportunity to change them, doing so in light of the new purpose statement can be impactful as it will show a full alignment between all pillars of the university. The vision can then be the dream of what can be achieved if the university lives by its purpose, and the mission can be a statement of commitment to go there. If the mission statement is too narrowly focused on being the best in the world and the purpose statement is about being best for the world (e.g. addressing society's greatest challenges), a misalignment could lead to a lack of legitimacy, trust and commitment.

> A purpose-driven university can rediscover its purpose by capturing its strengths and current and possible impact, and by connecting the two to reveal what it is that the university is already doing and what else it can do to become more purposeful and impactful.

Holistic Implementation

It seems like the natural next stage is implementation. We first set the goal, and then we expend effort to achieve it. However, two points need to be emphasised. First, even at this stage, it may be necessary to return to the previous stages. It is crucial to continue nurturing alliances and weaving the connections between the purpose allies at all stages. It is also essential to go back to any stakeholders or stakeholder groups who have not taken an active part in rediscovering the purpose, and present it to them. Their feedback and input could be invaluable.

Second, the purpose cannot remain as a mere statement, appearing on the website and under 'strategic planning'. It cannot be a marketing strategy or a PR exercise. Impact purpose does not exist unless it truly helps the person or organisation to create impact, and impact cannot be fully created if purpose is not embedded in every aspect of the organisation. To put it bluntly, the holistic approach is the differentiator between being impactful and being deceptive.

As such, holistic implementation includes examining and sometimes changing the way we evaluate research, teaching and service, on both the individual and organisational levels. A holistic approach requires an analysis of the way we work with every stakeholder group and how we can improve it to create social impact. It is about the university's environmental footprint and its contribution to society. In other words, it is about every aspect of academic and organisational life and how the university can help to reduce harm and make a real contribution.

Below is a list of possible purpose-led initiatives which may be used to instigate a multi-stakeholder conversation regarding holistic implementation. In a way, it summarises many points already raised in previous chapters, while also adding some new ideas. The list is not exclusive, and there may be many other initiatives which can be included at this stage. Its primary purpose is to show how many different aspects of the organisation may be affected by the new purpose and aid in achieving it. Again, many of these aspects may already be in place and, with some work and collaboration, they may be rediscovered, while others require new initiatives.

Holistic Purpose Implementation: List of Possible Initiatives

Purpose-Driven Teaching

- Mapping purpose-creating units, courses and programmes in the curriculum (e.g. corporate social responsibility, climate change and action, gender equity). Adding more courses and units related to impact, such as social/environmental consciousness and awareness, responsible leadership, or equality and equity issues.
- Aligning the curriculum with the SDGs and reporting on SDG-led teaching.
- Assessing teaching impact in terms of changes in students' lives and the impact they create in others.

- Measuring graduate attributes such as citizenship, ethics, prosocial activity and lifelong learning. Shifting from measuring graduate income to graduate impact.
- Creating service-learning and volunteering opportunities for all students, and employee volunteering opportunities for all staff, that genuinely contribute to society, not-for-profit organisations and the community.
- **A bold idea**: enabling students to teach their peers in the developing world. At Bentley University, students teach English via Skype to students in Afghanistan.

Impactful Research

- Measuring research impact, not in citation numbers but in terms of the impact it creates on people's quality of life, the wellbeing of the planet, community resilience and similar impact terms.
- Mapping research activities according to the SDGs and the purpose statement of the university.
- Creating research collaborations with other universities, corporate partners and additional stakeholders to address urgent issues, such as poverty and climate change.
- Recruiting and selecting lecturers and professors based on value alignment, purpose congruence and their ability to contribute to the new impact purpose through their research and teaching.
- Promoting people based on all aspects of scholarship (Boyer, 1990) and including aspects of social impact, good citizenship and contribution to society as part of the criteria.
- **A bold idea**: Using research capacity to fight poverty and provide social innovation to tackle society's greatest problems, like Stanford University with its Center for Social Innovation and its journal, *Stanford Social Innovation Review*.

Stakeholder Integration

- Identifying all the purpose-related stakeholders and integrating them into the purpose strategy.
- Working with internal stakeholders, including students, academic and professional staff, and university leadership to rediscover and achieve the purpose.
- Building alliances with external stakeholders to create new/additional impact.
- Enabling and encouraging all individuals to state their purpose and work towards it. Enabling people to live a purposeful life while studying or working at the university (see the *I Will* campaign by Erasmus University).
- Being a fair employer to all internal stakeholders, academic and professional staff alike. Leading gender equity strategy, supporting LGBTQ+ employees and creating fair opportunities for all.

- Creating partnerships with leading organisations such as government, the United Nations (including the UN Global Compact, SDSN and other agencies), multinational corporations and not-for-profit organisations to create a collective impact.
- **A bold idea**: working with the United Nations to address the urgent issue of refugees around the world, using the university's campuses to host refugees or sending academic staff to teach in refugee camps around the world. Columbia University does remarkable work with and for refugees.

Environmental Sustainability

- Working towards zero carbon emissions and zero waste, not only on the university's campuses but also within the enterprises the university works with and invests in.
- Investing in renewable energy and innovative solutions, creating green campuses and buildings and reducing the environmental footprint to the bare minimum.
- Using research and teaching to contribute to climate action, creating consultancy agencies to help other organisations to reduce their negative environmental impact and increase their positive one.
- **A bold idea**: The University of Illinois at Chicago (UIC) has committed to diverting 90% of landfill-bound material through techniques such as source reduction, materials reuse, recycling and composting. UIC plans an on-site facility for food waste recovery, such as food scrap composting, anaerobic digestion and waste-to-energy generation.

Social Responsibility and Ethics

- Developing holistic and in-depth ethical training for all staff, students and academic leaders, so that everyone involved with the university acts ethically and responsibly.
- Leading roundtables to discuss ethical issues for academia in general and the university in particular.
- Behaving in a way that does not harm local communities and society at large but instead contributes to people's wellbeing. Strengthening the local community can help create new partnerships and increase the number of local students.
- Aligning the university's giving (including staff giving) of time, money and knowledge with its strategy (purpose, mission, vision and values), thus avoiding 'random acts of charity'.
- Exhibiting zero tolerance to unethical and harmful behaviour, including corruption, sexual harassment, racism, bullying and fraud.
- **A bold idea**: Drexel University is working to bring the community in which it operates, West Philadelphia, out of poverty. Its West Philadelphia Promise

Zone is a programme delivered with the aim of identifying opportunities for community health improvement and providing interventions, from early education to high-school graduate internships.

Holistic implementation is not limited to this list, and it requires working on all possible aspects of being a purpose-driven university – socially, environmentally and ethically – in all activities: teaching, research, service and beyond.

> A purpose-driven university holistically implements its purpose. For a purpose-driven university, nothing is enough. It is not interested in giving a fish or teaching people how to fish. It won't rest until it revolutionises the fishing industry. For this, it needs to take a holistic approach where teaching, research, service and every other aspect of the university become an opportunity for impact.

Leading Impact

Impact is at the core of purpose and the concept of the purpose-driven university. It is the primary goal of writing this book. The impact can serve as the lighthouse towards which the academic ship is aiming; a beacon of light which determines all other academic activities.

A purpose-driven university must define the social impact it aims to create through its strengths and unique value proposition as part of its vision, mission statement and purpose. Ideally, the impact then becomes a core component of every policy and action, every report and event, and the university's culture and story. This is what is meant by 'leading impact', not just 'creating impact', and, by doing so, the university can become a leader in the market, paving the way for other universities to do the same. Leading impact and leading with impact also imply that it is the task of all the formal and informal leaders of the purpose-driven university, working with moral courage and a vision to use the university's power and resources to benefit others.

Leading impact implies that the university shifts away from only considering rankings of excellence, such as that of the regular THE (*Times Higher Education*), to also consider rankings of impact and sustainability, such as the THE Impact Ranking or green campuses ranking. It means a transformation in how we measure academic success, shifting away from indicators such as graduate income to graduate impact. Instead of examining how much our alumni make, we should evaluate the difference they make: Have they become social entrepreneurs? Have they started a not-for-profit organisation? Are they leading a business with a higher purpose? Are they using the knowledge gained in our university to increase people's wellbeing? We need to also change the focus of the university from impact factors to real societal impact. It is not that universities should not encourage their academic staff to publish in top-tier journals; they should. However, they should also encourage scholars to focus, aim for and report on the impact that their publications have had on others, such as on industry, policymakers and community organisations. Academics might also assess whether their research was implemented in any way to create a positive impact. Of course, these data are more difficult to find, but if scholars have this in mind while writing and publishing, they may also collect and find evidence of impact. Many academics and scholars have such evidence but are never asked to consider it, let alone exhibit it.

As such, leading impact may result in changing the way we measure the KPIs (key performance indicators) of the organisation, its leaders and employees. The purpose of the KPIs is to enable measurement of individual and organisational performance (Chan & Chan, 2004). As KPIs are general indicators of performance that focus on critical aspects of outputs or outcomes, a purpose-driven university makes social impact a critical aspect of expected outcomes. KPIs should always relate to the overall mission and, as such, to purpose and impact purpose. Particularly concerning purpose, there needs to be a commitment and engagement. Thus, KPIs should be based on conversations and mutual agreement.

Leading impact requires a good understanding and use of social impact assessment frameworks, such as the theory of change, the basic programme logic and social return on investment (see Chapter 6). The theory of change could assist universities in leading impact, as impact becomes the goal of the entire process. After setting it, the university could work backwards on the desired outcomes and activities to also understand the resources (financial, human and intellectual capitals) needed to achieve its impact.

As mentioned in other parts of the book, to measure impact the university needs to continuously collect and analyse data regarding positive and negative impacts, both intended and unintended. In some cases, the data already exist within the university, and all that is required is the affirmative decision and action to focus on it, whereas, in other cases, new data collection is necessary. It is vital not to wait until the time is ripe for reporting but to collect these data as soon as the decision is made to move in the direction of a purpose-driven university, as it can assist in making the process more effective and efficient.

Indeed, collecting data on impact can assist at all stages of the purpose-driven university framework. As it is a circular model in which organisations will go back and forth, data can better inform decision-makers on building alliances, weaving connections, rediscovering purpose, and on the effectiveness of holistic implementation.

> A purpose-driven university leads with impact, as impact becomes its reason for being. It collects data and stories about the impact created by the university and about the collective impact created with partners. Purpose and impact become the litmus test of the performance of the individual and the organisation.

Sharing

Sharing is a critical stage, yet not many universities, even purpose-driven universities, do it well. This step is about sharing – the impact, the story and the learnings so that the university can become more purpose-driven, position itself as such and so that others can learn from it and be inspired by it.

We need to share the impact assessment done in Step 5 above. Universities can use mixed methods, combining statistical indicators and analysis with compelling stories of individuals, groups and communities. It is crucial not only to report on the impact of the university but also on the collective impact it creates with others. Sharing impact contributes to the university's transparency, accountability and responsibility.

These indicators of impact can be integrated to share the inspirational story of the university. The university can tell its story of how it became purpose-driven and how it engaged allies in the journey towards purpose. It can also share those stories of making a difference it discovered and created. Universities can tell a narrative of outstanding volunteering, of human courage and compassion, and of empowering others to take control of their lives, while becoming a change agent in the community. People, including students and staff, are keen to hear inspirational stories and engage in them.

A purpose-driven university needs also to share the learning it gains from the process of becoming. The history of the university, coupled with its story of working for the community, is engaging. However, this is not just about successes and positive impact. It is also essential to reflect on and share the related obstacles, hurdles and difficulties so that others may learn from them and realise that it can be hard for others too. If an Ivy League university struggles with leading a change towards impact, smaller universities may find the courage to do so. Reflective practice is an integral part of any change process but particularly when the aim is to become 'best for the world'. Reflective practice undertaken by and with a university's stakeholders can also lead to engagement and integration.

> Sharing is how the university can become a leader among other higher education institutions, especially those who care about impact and purpose. Sharing is how the university itself can become better at it. Sharing does not mean that the work is done. Usually it means it has just begun.

Imperative Questions to Ask

The purpose-driven university model offers steps and suggestions for beginning the journey towards purpose and for a holistic, multi-stakeholder implementation. There are three questions to ask here:

(1) *What stages in this process are crucial?* Each university will be placed at a different stage in the journey towards purpose. Some are only beginning to reflect on the possibilities involved in purpose, while others have already mapped things out and worked with their stakeholders. Others still already lead with purpose. Each university will need to recognise at what stage it needs to begin the process, while ensuring no steps are skipped just for convenience or lack of resources.

(2) *Who should be involved at each stage?* While Stage 1 and Stage 2 require as many stakeholders as possible, and certain individuals may undertake the next four stages, it is essential to establish who would 'own' each stage and take responsibility for it, and who else should be involved at each stage. For some universities, the answer may be everyone, whereas, for others, some stages will be led by smaller groups. There are benefits and challenges related to each option, and the more inclusive the process is, the more engaged people will be with the change.

(3) *How do we ensure the process remains circular and active?* The journey towards purpose is never-ending. It is not as if one finds a purpose, delivers on it and the process thus concludes. If we aim to live a purposeful life and work in a purposeful organisation, the process is never fully completed for as long as the individual or the organisation is alive. However, it takes effort and action to ensure the continuity of the process, with people taking ownership and responsibility to keep working on each stage and drive the full process through.

References

Aspen Institute. (2019). *Weave the social fabric project.* Retrieved from www.aspeninstitute.org/programs/weave-the-social-fabric-initiative

Boyer, E. L. (1990). *Scholarship reconsidered: Priorities of the professoriate.* Lawrenceville, NJ: Princeton University Press.

Chan, A., & Chan, A. (2004). Key performance indicators for measuring construction success. *Benchmarking: An International Journal, 11*(2), 203–221.

Chapter 9

The Way Forward in Higher Education

Innovation and Forward-thinking at KU Leuven University

Bioscience engineers from KU Leuven's Centre for Surface Chemistry and Catalysis recently invented a new generation of solar panels that can efficiently produce hydrogen gas out of thin air. In another project, researchers managed to develop an alternative way to preserve an entire banana collection for ages. Using liquid nitrogen at a temperature of −196°C, small pieces of each banana variety's growing tips are frozen and kept. Even after hundreds of years, these samples can be unfrozen and regenerated into a new viable plant to address food insecurity. In 2018, KU Leuven ranked seventh on Thomson Reuters' list of the World's Most Innovative Universities, the highest-ranking of any university outside the USA. KU Leuven says it is an institution for research and education, where all programmes are based on innovative research (KU Leuven, 2019a).

Founded in 1425 by Pope Martin V, KU Leuven is the world's oldest Catholic University. Part of KU's modern mission is to conduct comprehensive and advanced scientific research. Based in Belgium's Flanders region, the Dutch-speaking University is open to students of all faiths. It operates autonomously from the Church and maintains one of the largest independent research and development organisations in the world. KU Leuven is dedicated to education and research through its 15 faculties, clustered into three groups: Humanities and Social Sciences; Science, Engineering and Technology (SET); and Biomedical Sciences.

Today, KU Leuven offers Massive Open Online Courses (MOOCs) via its channel on edX, with more than 150,000 learners from 175 countries. Free online courses include topics such as ecosystems and biodiversity, existential wellbeing and human rights. In addition, the University is involved in open education by publishing a number of course units as OpenCourseWare (OCW). KU Leuven says its focus is on course units which (can) appeal to a broader audience and multiple disciplines. The University also offers blended learning opportunities (combining online learning with face-to-face classroom experiences) and 'flipped classrooms' – delivering instructional content online and moving activities, such as homework, into the classroom.

KU Leuven also does some work around sustainability and purpose. The University has a 10-point plan for sustainability, including offering a MOOC on sustainability to new students, selling sustainable food in the cafeterias and reducing its carbon emissions. KU Leuven also leads the Leuven Sustainability Institute (LSI):

Conservation and efficiency gains will be the focus of this institute, apart from advanced technological research on new solutions. The LSI will have the resources to achieve this mission. Interdisciplinary research into sustainability will receive the necessary attention. We consider the development of research and education in low-income countries to be an important contribution to a sustainable global society (KU Leuven, 2019b).

An innovative model of integrating research and purpose is 'Metaforum', KU Leuven's interdisciplinary think tank that aims to bring together existing scholarship and scientific expertise to address various societal issues. It works on issues such as society and democracy, economic and social policy, nature and ecology, and reflections on university and science.

Introduction

When I did my first degree nearly 30 years ago, students had a schedule that they went by, running from one classroom to the next. In each classroom or lecture theatre, there stood a professor, usually a man, who put slides in the overhead or slide projector, and talked for 90 minutes straight. This professor professed in his or her area of expertise and it was therefore legitimate to share a small part of this knowledge with the 'not-so-knowledgeable' students. Students concentrated on taking notes, and a few brave students would ask a question. At the end of each semester, we students would take an exam to test how well we had memorised these notes we were taking. Most of this knowledge will have escaped the students a year later. Such an experience probably sounds familiar to most people who are reading this book – professors or university leaders who studied a few decades ago. However, things are changing rapidly.

The emerging literature on the future of higher education is mainly preoccupied with innovation and digitalisation, student-centred education and financial security. The issues faced by higher education vary by country: in Australia, there is a concern surrounding governmental funding for universities, whereas, in the USA, higher education institutions are troubled by student numbers and access to knowledge in the digital age. Universities all around the world are shifting to online, virtual and experiential learning; to an emphasis on innovation and artificial intelligence (AI); and to novel teaching methods. Concerned with funding and student demand, universities are preparing themselves for the future, which is understandable. However, what this discourse is missing is a few burning questions: What can higher education institutions do in the face of climate change? How is the nature of work changing with automation and AI, and what are the implications for society and higher education? How can we help prepare a new generation of students to address these and other crucial issues?

The future of higher education should be more closely tied to the future of work, the future of this planet and the future of humanity. A disconnect between higher education and these issues could lead to detachment, illegitimacy and irrelevance. This chapter will cover emerging ideas on the future of higher education and the future of purpose, to conclude this book with the future of the purpose-driven university and an epilogue.

The Future of Higher Education

> The best way to predict the future is to create it. (Abraham Lincoln)

Over the last two decades, many universities have undergone some major transformations, some of which were internally driven by higher education institutions while others were forced upon them by market disrupters and global changes. With the growth of MOOCs, new learning methods, and increased financial and sustainability pressures, the higher education landscape is rapidly altering (Lukanic, 2014). University leaders all around the world are engaging in new strategies to leverage these emerging challenges and opportunities. Institutions which only rely on their history and past success may start lagging behind and become irrelevant. Long-standing models of higher education that prefer tradition and stability will be replaced or even displaced by new approaches that embrace innovation, connectivity and meaningfulness.

According to Mintz (2013), we are in the midst of a new higher education revolution with many well-known forces at play: economic, demographic, market-driven and ideological. Higher education must address a host of criticisms regarding graduation rates, levels of student engagement, learning outcomes, employability and value for money.

The Nature of Teaching in Higher Education

One major transformation in higher education is in the way universities teach, shifting away from the face-to-face lecture model. From online teaching, MOOCs, flipped classrooms, blended learning and experiential education to service-learning and mindful learning, university teaching is increasingly occurring outside the classroom. Students also bring rich knowledge and experience into the classroom, resulting in shared learning.

In addition, academic curricula are predicted to become more multidisciplinary. Lukanic (2014) argues that our current models, in which the curriculum is developed and fostered independent of the university at large, must change. Students demand cross-disciplinary learning and thinking, particularly in science, engineering and technology. As such, universities must think about the ways in which space and structure need to change to serve interdisciplinary curricula. For example, the University of Utah is developing a transformative entrepreneurial building where students can create and launch companies in the same space.

Higher Education in the Digital Age

The digital revolution is often at the base of the discussion on the future of higher education. According to Tate (2017), AI, analytics, augmented, virtual reality, robotic telepresence and cyber defence will be the driving forces in digital learning at colleges and universities over the next 20 years. Big data and data interpretation will also become centrepieces of higher education, while technology advancement will help instructors begin to focus more on the application of learning rather than the acquisition of knowledge.

Indeed, many journal articles on the future of higher education predict that a substantial part of learning will be done online. The question is – what can universities offer in an age where knowledge is so accessible? One-way streaming of knowledge cannot be it, as it can be easily replaced by search engines, MOOCs and even AI. If a robot or a computer can replace a professor, maybe this professor should not be teaching in a university in the first place. We need to move to experiential, meaningful and mindful learning, where the interaction is not just a necessity; it is an advantage. Many universities featured in this book, from Stanford University in the first chapter to KU Leuven in the last, demonstrate an innovative way of teaching. Even in the digital age, people still want to interact, and innovative universities can offer a meaningful way of doing so. Online learning can also be highly interactive and enjoyable, using innovative technologies to split an online class into syndicate groups, and to create brainstorming platforms and in-depth discussions. We have only begun to utilise the immense potential of virtual reality, for example, to offer innovative experiential learning, which could use distance learning but enable the students to feel that they are on campus or in the field.

Some universities are applying the most cutting-edge technologies to disrupt higher education and transform platforms and teaching. Blockchain offers innovative ways to use secured data in universities, but only a few universities are taking advantage of it. The University of Melbourne started using blockchain to issue digital credentials and enabled students to share verified copies of their qualifications with potential employers. Moore (2019) offered four ways in which universities can apply blockchain in higher education: (1) improve record keeping; (2) increase efficiency in existing business processes; (3) create a new market for digital assets and (4) create a disruptive business model. For example, Woolf University aims to become the first blockchain-powered, not-for-profit and borderless university. Founded by academics from Oxford and Cambridge, Woolf will rely on blockchain and smart contracts as the basis of the relationship between learners and educators, while borrowing ideas from the sharing economy.

Student-centred Higher Education

Another element that seems to be a reoccurring theme in the articles and books on the future of higher education is a student-driven higher education. Students' demand for high-quality, engaging and useful education will change universities.

Lukanic (2014) explains that the common denominator amidst the recent changes in higher education is the students:

> To best recruit and retain students, universities need to evaluate how they offer a student life experience that prepares students to be healthy and dynamic people in the future. That means universities need to embrace sustainability and wellness as key components of campus life.

Mintz (2013) also agrees that the most crucial challenge of higher education today is the shift in the way students consume knowledge and gain a degree. Instead of attending a single institution, students can receive credit in multiple ways, including from early-college/dual-degree programmes, community colleges, online providers and multiple universities. Students may embrace online education while undermining core curricula, which served as a cash cow for universities. Many students now choose micro-credentials instead of a full degree, to meet their learning goals and to stay updated in a rapidly changing job market. A purpose-driven university can offer such experiences that are also meaningful to the students throughout their education and their careers.

Employability in the Era of AI

Edservice (2018) produced an infographic on higher education in 2025, predicting that students will require tangible results in the shape of post-graduation jobs. With the growing population and atomisation of the workplace, not everyone will be able to find a job. Harari (2017) claims that soon we might witness the most unequal society in history, as a growing number of people will be 'useless' and unable to work. This implies that universities may need to reflect on the kind of skills and competencies students will require in the future, and why learning through memorising will not be effective in today's job market, as much as learning by analysing and creativity. Higher education institutions need to help students develop their entrepreneurial aptitude so that they can become job creators (for themselves and others) instead of just job seekers. We are shifting to a lifelong learning model, replacing the three-year degree model.

Collaborations and Partnerships

The future of higher education is anchored in collaboration rather than competition. Selingo (2017) argued that we should acknowledge that not-for-profit education is tax-exempt because it is supposed to be a common good, rather than a business fighting for turf. As such, 'the time for going it alone has ended'. Selingo's concept is the 'networked university', where shared structures capitalise on each university's strengths and multiple institutions link to reduce expenses while delivering essential services. While Selingo is mainly focusing here on collaboration for financial benefit, universities can also collaborate on goals of sustainability, purpose and collective impact, as will be detailed below.

The above changes present an exceptional opportunity for innovation and disruption. In an article in *Stanford Social Innovation Review*, Gilbert, Crow, and Anderson (2018) recommended that universities use design thinking to reconstruct their core functions, while also creating the capacity to reach emerging and underserved markets. A design perspective suggests that there are architectural choices to be made about what the university seeks to accomplish and how it is organised to achieve those ends. A dual transformation design strategy has proved especially effective for addressing both legacy and emerging markets. Here, operations act in parallel: one to develop strategies that optimise the core organisation to become more responsive to new demands, while the second aims to design and implement disruptive innovations that provide a basis for future growth, agility and responsivity.

Universities need to become more entrepreneurial, virtual, innovative, flexible, student-oriented and collaborative. Given that the changes listed in this section may transform universities beyond recognition, several new universities emerge based on novel models and structures. For example, Quest University in Canada has no faculty ranks, no tenure and no departments (Helfand, 2011). Teaching is central to its mission, and all staff share the teaching task equally. The faculty's work is a combination of teaching, scholarship, curriculum development and service, individually tailored according to needs and capabilities. Helfand (2011) asserted that this collegial approach fosters academic freedom, creative collaboration and engagement.

The question remains – how can these changes and shifts be used in a university that does not only want to innovate and grow, but also to create a positive impact and address societal issues? All of these changes and others can be used to achieve the impact a purpose-driven university aims at. The next section will, therefore, cover the future of purpose to discuss how the meaning of being a purpose-driven organisation is also changing.

The Future of Purpose

This section examines the issues that are likely to be the foci of purpose-driven organisations. As impact purpose is closely related to the issues discussed in this book, such as sustainability, social impact and responsible leadership, it is essential to explain how the focus and implementation of these issues are changing. Hence, the way that such ideas and concepts could materialise in the next few years will be discussed, as they could also affect the purpose-driven university. Based on the most recent literature and trends in CSR and purpose-driven organisations, below are four possible and prominent developments in the area of purpose, responsibility and sustainability.

Holistic Approach

In recent years, CSR has shifted from being a business sideshow with a limited focus on philanthropy to a holistic approach on how a business operates throughout the entire value chain. An increasing number of leading companies understand that it is no longer sufficient to communicate how good they are for the community; they need to embed responsibility and sustainability in every aspect of their business. In August 2019, the Business Roundtable announced the release of a new 'Statement on the Purpose of a Corporation'. Over 180 CEOs signed it and committed to lead their companies for the benefit of all stakeholders and to adopt a holistic and multi-stakeholder approach to doing so (Business Roundtable, 2019). Consumers, employees and other stakeholders do not respond positively to companies who do not 'walk the talk', criticising such decoupling as 'greenwashing' and expressing similar condemnations, which lead to a lack of trust.

The holistic approach is now expected from business and other types of organisations from all sectors of the economy, such as governments, public service, not-for-profit organisations, social enterprises and higher education institutions. If an organisation claims to create a public good, it needs to demonstrate how it does that without harming others (humans, animals and the planet) while delivering on its promises. An organisation cannot create harm on the one hand (e.g. using modern slavery) to create a positive social impact on the other hand (e.g. give money to charity), without the risk of illegitimacy.

The holistic approach has been discussed several times in this book, particularly in Chapters 3 and 8, and it can be embedded in universities which aim to be purpose-led. It implies transforming teaching, research, engagement, governance, promotion, recruitment, student bodies and anything else that makes a university what it is, so these are all leveraged to create a positive impact in the community and in society.

Environmental Issues: Climate Change

There are not many journal articles discussing the future of sustainability and CSR which ignore the increasing urgency of climate change and how it is going to impact every aspect of our personal and organisational life. As the effects of climate change impact an increasing number of countries, people and organisations, they become a crucial issue in the future of purpose.

Climate change is defined as 'a change in global or regional climate patterns, in particular, a change apparent from the mid to late 20th century onwards and attributed largely to the increased levels of atmospheric carbon dioxide produced by the use of fossil fuels' (OECD, 2017). The Fourth Assessment Report addressed any doubts regarding climate change by the IPCC in 2007 (Parry, Canziani, Palutikof, van der Linden, & Hanson, 2007). The impact of climate change is yet to be fully apprehended, but we can already see a sharp incline in extreme weather, extreme temperatures and the number of natural disasters.

According to the Australian Academy of Science (2015), the most explicit present-day impacts of climate change can be seen in the natural environment, with warming temperatures and heatwaves. These, in turn, affect the biodiversity of the planet. Some of these changes directly affect human activities, such as food and water scarcity, health, infrastructure and basic livelihood, due to natural disasters and the inability to live in extreme conditions. Climate change will affect migration, the economy and political regimes.

Furthermore, the impacts of climate change often act to amplify other stresses, including urban encroachment, fragmentation, deforestation, invasive species, warfare and civil unrest, overpopulation, poverty and sinking land. Multiple stresses do not merely add to each other; they cascade together in unexpected ways. Therefore, climate change impacts, interacting with other stresses, have the potential to shift some ecosystems and societies into new states, with significant consequences for human wellbeing and the survival of the planet and its ecosystem (Australian Academy of Science, 2015).

These issues have a different effect on various types of organisation in different countries. Governments may be occupied with policy, financial aid and global commitment to control carbon emissions and rising temperatures. Businesses are more likely to examine the ways in which climate change and natural disasters may impact the economy, their supply chains and risk mitigation.

For universities, climate change will have all the aforementioned effects but may also impact on their ability to attract students and teachers, particularly from and in some global regions. Many universities are involved in climate research (e.g. the Cambridge Centre for Climate Science), deliver courses and programmes on climate change, and partner with other organisations to lead conferences, roundtables and academic debates. Some universities take more significant action to combat climate change through pledging zero carbon emissions, refitting buildings to be more energy-efficient and engaging students and staff. Wageningen University & Research (WUR) in the Netherlands has a mission 'to explore the potential of nature to improve the quality of life'. WUR leads research projects and activities in energy, waste and mobility and aims to reduce its climate impact by producing its own renewable energy. The University of British Columbia has a climate action plan ('Climate Action 2020') to reduce greenhouse gas emissions by 100% by 2050, to use the university as a lab to develop climate change solutions, and to take full responsibility for its impact on the environment and related costs. Inspired and led by Greta Thunberg, students and academic staff all around the world participated in the climate strikes in 2019, whereas in some universities, such as at the University of Nottingham, staff and students went on a strike for climate action. Students at RMIT University in Australia were even offered full marks on part of an environmental design project for attending the climate strike.

Environmental issues will prevail in the next two decades, and purpose-driven universities need to consider how they can help to address them. Universities can help mitigate climate change and its impact and discover solutions, through research and development.

Innovative Ways to Communicate with and Engage Stakeholders

As stakeholder integration is becoming more prevalent for businesses and universities alike (see Chapter 5), purpose-driven organisations find innovative ways and opportunities to work with various stakeholder groups in order to jointly achieve impact purpose. While there are many stakeholder groups and opportunities to involve them all, here the focus will be on consumers and employees in purpose-driven business, and students and academic staff in universities.

In purpose-driven companies, such innovative means include consumer engagement in creating social impact. Some companies involve their consumers in giving money to causes, in volunteering for charities they partner with and to help them to become more sustainable. Optus, a telecom company in Australia (and a subsidiary of Singtel in Singapore), allows some of its customers to donate unused data to charities. Thankyou, a social enterprise selling products such as bottled water and toiletries to address societal issues in the developing world, has a social impact tracker on each product so consumers can see the location of the project they helped to support. Companies can use big data to create social impact and utilise new platforms of communication to involve consumers in addressing society's most significant challenges.

Similarly, there are innovative ways and opportunities to involve employees in achieving purpose. Some companies have recently begun to enable employees to initiate and lead purpose-related projects. An emerging term is social intrapreneurship where an entrepreneurial employee develops a profitable new product, service or business model to create value for society (Jenkins, 2018). Research shows that cognitive, network and cultural embeddedness all play a vital role in social intrapreneurship (Kistruck & Beamish, 2010).

For universities, there are remarkable opportunities to use emerging innovation and engage their students and staff in their purpose. Using digital platforms to involve students and staff in purpose can be impactful. Erasmus University in the Netherlands encourages students, staff and university leadership to declare their purpose through the I WILL campaign (see Chapter 2). When people commit to purpose statements, the entire university becomes more purpose-driven. Universities can use novel digital platforms such as Coursera to provide potential, current, past or external students with micro-credentials and short courses on human rights, climate action or CSR, at low or no cost. Such online education can also be used as a way to continuously engage with alumni and involve them in purpose, beyond asking for donations. Students can also become social entrepreneurs, creating a business that addresses a social or environmental problem, with the support of the university, its incubator and partnerships. I developed a Master of Social Entrepreneurship at Macquarie University (the first one in Australia and only one of a few such programmes in the world), in which students learned how to develop and scale a social enterprise to serve society.

Future of Work

Two years ago, I attended a conference with a keynote address by the CEO of one of the largest multinational delivery service companies. I asked him how his company is preparing for delivery by drones and self-driving cars, and whether the firm's CSR will determine job replacement in the next decade. His answer was somewhat surprising: 'this is not going to happen', he said. Imagine the CEO of a supermarket chain saying that self-checkouts are not going to happen.

Everyone needs to be prepared for the fast-changing nature of work – it is due diligence. With the prediction that automation, robots, machine learning and AI will replace many current jobs, scholars and practitioners strive to predict the impact of this on organisations, economies and livelihoods. A study of 46 countries and 800 occupations by the McKinsey Global Institute found that robot automation will take over 800 million jobs by 2030, implying that up to one-fifth of the global workforce will be affected (BBC, 2017). According to an OECD report (2019), in the next few years, 14% of current jobs will be completely automated, and another 32% will change significantly. In addition, an increasing number of people are earning their income nowadays through the gig economy (e.g. Airtasker) and the sharing economy (e.g. Airbnb and Uber).

What a purpose-driven organisation can do is to help employees prepare for this future and create an employer policy. It needs to decide whether the company will continue to employ people who can be replaced by a machine, as a strategy and a policy. It may not be the best short-term policy financially, but it could create a strong culture and connectedness within companies that value human capital. Some companies gain consumer support and loyalty by choosing their employees over AI and automation. Some firms are already preparing their employees for the day they might lose their job to a machine or robot. They do so by providing them with new skills to allow them to find a new role within the organisation, or another job elsewhere.

In the same vein, universities will need to prepare their students for such a future. It is not enough to develop students' employability and competencies for the current job market – universities need to prepare them for tomorrow. This goes beyond providing students with digital skills; it is about developing lifelong learning, resilience, a flexible mindset and creativity. As mentioned, students will need to develop their entrepreneurial spirit and intrapreneurial skills to succeed in tomorrow's workplace.

At the same time, a purpose-driven university needs to concern itself with the job security of its employees. It is not only professional staff who may lose their jobs due to automation but academic staff as well. With the shift to virtual learning, the model of a lecturer standing in front of a class may significantly change. Yuki, the first robot lecturer, was introduced in Germany in 2019 and has already started delivering lectures to university students at the Philipps University of Marburg. Many academics believe that, due to the creative aspects of their research and writing, they will not be replaced by AI, but this is not the case. In 2019, the academic publisher Springer Nature unveiled the first research book generated using machine learning. The book, *Lithium-Ion Batteries: A Machine-generated Summary of Current Research*, is a summary of peer-reviewed papers published on the topic in question. Machines can generate literature reviews and even empirical data analysis and may soon write academic papers. The role of academic research may alter, and universities need to help prepare academic staff to do work that is not replaceable by a computer.

However, AI cannot work with compassion to use its teaching and research to create a positive impact in the world (at least not yet). Leading a purpose-driven university and creating a sense of meaningfulness among academic staff could be the key to creating an academic workforce that is not so easily replaceable.

The Future of the Purpose-Driven University and Closing Remarks

Based on Carroll (2015), we can offer three scenarios on the purpose-driven university: the gloomy scenario, the probable scenario and the hopeful scenario. *The gloomy scenario* suggests that, in the future, universities will continue with 'business as usual' – focusing only on teaching and research without an emphasis on social impact and continuing to concentrate on ranking, profits and graduate income. Sustainability and social responsibility will disappear as a fading trend, and universities will focus on the next trend to continuously increase student intake, donations, research outputs and teaching excellence.

The probable scenario implies some level of purpose, responsibility and sustainability, with perhaps an increase in the number of universities that attend to societal and environmental issues. Sustainability and social responsibility will be a 'nice to have' marginal aspect of universities. There may be some sustainability and social impact reports and efforts, but they will not lead the strategy of higher education institutions. Purpose will not be the major driver of higher education, but it may affect certain aspects of academic life.

The hopeful scenario is very optimistic, with higher education institutions changing their approach, their role in society and their core operations. Here, universities are not only as sustainable as some companies and not-for-profit organisations but they even lead the way. In the hopeful scenario, this book will become obsolete because every university in the world will be purpose-driven. University leaders will work with students, staff and all other stakeholders to create a positive impact in the world, leveraging their power, resources, people, intellect and campuses to make a substantial contribution to society. In the hopeful scenario, universities will no longer care about being the best in the world; they will care about being the best *for* the world.

This book was written with hope, so I want to believe that the hopeful scenario is not impossible. The book is based on reimagining what higher education could be – purposeful, impactful and meaningful. It is not likely that the book will be obsolete because every university is purpose-driven. Neither do I think it will be obsolete because no one will use it either. It is possible that an increasing number of universities, their leaders, teachers and students will use this book and similar ones to lead universities with a robust impact purpose.

To be better prepared for the future, university leaders and staff must know what the future holds – the future of higher education *and* the future of purpose – in order to lead a purpose-driven university that is future-ready. Integrating ideas and trends from the future of higher education, such as digitalisation of education, together with shifts surrounding purpose, such as environmental issues, can lead to innovative solutions. For example, universities could use digital platforms to connect students in the developed world with students from a university in the developing world to jointly collaborate on climate action. Universities could address employability while also developing students' global mindset, entrepreneurial skills and good citizenship. Doing so will not only provide students with a job but will also help them to create an impactful social enterprise that can change the world. The five aspects of the future of higher education (and others) can be combined with the four aspects of the future of purpose (and others) to provide imaginative and novel solutions to the most difficult challenges humanity is facing today.

References

Australian Academy of Science. (2015). *What are the impacts of climate change?* Retrieved from www.science.org.au/learning/general-audience/science-climate-change/7-what-are-impacts-of-climate-change

BBC. (2017). *Robot automation will 'take 800 million jobs by 2030' – report.* Retrieved from www.bbc.com/news/world-us-canada-42170100

Business Roundtable. (2019). *Our commitment.* Retrieved from www.opportunity.businessroundtable.org/ourcommitment

Carroll, A. B. (2015). Corporate social responsibility. *Organizational Dynamics, 44*(2), 87–96.

Edservice. (2018). *2025 Future state of higher education infographic.* Retrieved from www.edservices.wiley.com/wp-content/uploads/2018/03/WES_2025-Future-State-of-Higher-Ed-Infographic_FINAL.pdf

Gilbert, C. G., Crow, M. M., & Anderson, D. (2018). Design thinking for higher education. *Stanford Social Innovation Review.* Retrieved from www.ssir.org/articles/entry/design_thinking_for_higher_education

Harari, N. Y. (2017, May 24). Are we about to witness the most unequal societies in history? *The Guardian.* Retrieved from www.theguardian.com/inequality/2017/may/24/are-we-about-to-witness-the-most-unequal-societies-in-history-yuval-noah-harari?CMP=Share_iOSApp_Other

Helfand, D. (2011). Higher education: Academic questions. *Nature, 477*(7363), 158.

Jenkins, B. (2018). Cultivating the social intrapreneur. *Stanford Social Innovation Review.* Retrieved from www.ssir.org/articles/entry/cultivating_the_social_intrapreneur

Kistruck, G. M., & Beamish, P. W. (2010). The interplay of form, structure, and embeddedness in social intrapreneurship. *Entrepreneurship Theory and Practice, 34*(4), 735–761.

KU Leuven. (2019a). *About KU Leuven.* Retrieved from www.kuleuven.be/english/about-kuleuven/

KU Leuven. (2019b). *Sustainability.* Retrieved from www.kuleuven.be/duurzaamheid/sustainability

Lukanic, B. (2014). Five bold predictions for the future of higher education: What, where, and how will we learn? *Fast Company.* Retrieved from www.fastcompany.com/3029109/5-bold-predictions-for-the-future-of-higher-education

Mintz, S. (2013). The future is now: 15 innovations to watch for. *The Chronicle of Higher Education.* Retrieved from www.chronicle.com/article/The-Future-Is-Now-15/140479

Moore, S. (2019). The most ambitious uses for blockchain in higher education could disrupt the industry. *Gartner*. Retrieved from www.gartner.com/smarterwithgartner/4-ways-blockchain-will-transform-higher-education/

OECD. (2017). *Glossary of statistical terms*. Retrieved from www.stats.oecd.org/glossary/detail.asp?ID=360

OECD. (2019). *Future of work*. Retrieved from www.oecd.org/els/emp/future-of work/data

Parry, M., Canziani, O., Palutikof, J., van der Linden, P., & Hanson, C. (2007). *Climate change 2007: Impacts, adaption and vulnerability*. Cambridge: Cambridge University Press.

Selingo, J. J. (2017). Networked U.'s: This is what will save higher ed. *The Chronicle of Higher Education*. Retrieved from www.chronicle.com/article/Networked-U-s-This-Is-What/241724

Tate, E. (2017). Digital learning leaders forecast the future of higher education. *Edscoop*. Retrieved from www.edscoop.com/digital-learning-leaders-forecast-the-future-of-higher-education

Epilogue

The time for the purpose-driven university movement is now. Business as usual for universities is no longer an option, as we are quickly losing our legitimacy and exposing ourselves to stakeholder pressure and disapproval. Universities can become a force for good, using their power to make a difference. If university leaders do not lead the way with purpose, students will do it from the bottom up, and they already are. Students all across the globe are starting organisations and movements to act on climate change, social inclusion, activism and impact purpose. It is time for academic leaders, staff and students to come together in each university to define their purpose and impact, take steps to achieve it and share an incredible story of impact with the world.

If we do this, we can change the narrative on universities from one of ivory towers and elitist institutions to that of purpose-driven and impactful agents for social change. I started the book with the top Google search results for 'Universities are'. I can imagine a day when the top search results will be more similar to those in Fig. E.1.

In the introduction to the book, I shared my personal story and journey, which began with the little boy I tutored over 20 years ago, and how this impact-creating activity and extra-curricular endeavour changed my life and my career. I have

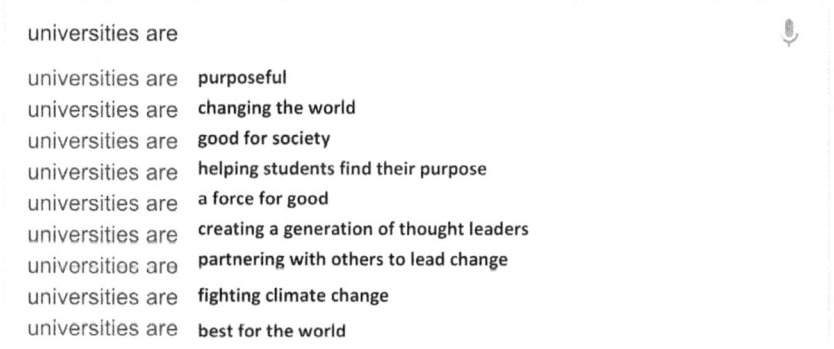

Fig. E.1. Imagine a Day: A Vision for Better Google Search Results.

recently found this 8-year-old boy. He may have been a fragile youngster, but he is no longer fragile today. He is a director of a leading IT company and a family man, with two children of his own. He still remembers me. My former university did not just educate me; it provided me with a life-changing opportunity to make a difference and to discover my own purpose, which I define as using my teaching, research and knowledge to create a positive impact in the world. This is what a purpose-driven university is all about.

Index

Academic jobs, 75–76
Academic leadership, 4, 53–63
Academic promotion, 49–50
Academic staff, employee engagement, 76–77
Admissions scandal, 38
Anti-discrimination policy, 38
Apple, 15–16
Appreciative inquiry, 107–109
Artificial intelligence (AI), 137, 142–143
Ashoka U Changemaker Campus, 36
Aspen Institute, 123
Association to Advance Collegiate Schools of Business (AACSB), 17
Australian Academy of Science, 139
Australian Research Council (ARC), 79

Ball, Deborah, 114
Ben & Jerry's, 3, 11, 29, 98
Bentley University, 77, 126
The Body Shop, 11, 29
Boston College (BC), 15
Boston University, 18
Boyer's Model of Scholarship, 45–46, 50
British Ministry of Education, 84
Brungs, Attila, 89
Building alliances, 121–122
Business Roundtable, 25, 139
Business–university partnerships, 79

Cambridge University, 41
Cause-related marketing, 98
Center for Social Innovation, 8
Center on Poverty and Inequality, 43
Charité-Universitätsmedizin Berlin, 18

Climate change, 41, 43, 72, 83, 84, 125, 139–140
Competency-based model, 74
Conscious capitalism, 40, 60, 119
Conscious leadership, 60–61, 119
Consumer engagement, 141
Cooperrider, David, 109
Cornell University, 18
    teaching philosophy, 47–48
Corporate partners, 79–82
Corporate social responsibility (CSR), 2, 4, 5, 106, 119, 138, 141
    defined, 36–37
Crane, Andrew, 47

Dalai Lama, 60, 109
Deloitte Millennial Survey, 72
Digital revolution, 136
Dove, 29
Drexel University, 30–31, 115, 127
Duke University, 18

Ecological environment, 84
Edelman, 29
Emotional intelligence (EQ), 60–61, 63, 75
Emotional learning, 109
Employability, 30, 48, 74–75, 82, 137, 142
Employee engagement, 26–29, 76–77
Employee volunteering, 38, 126
Enactus, 24, 74
Enron, 19
Entrepreneurial leadership. *See also* Leadership, 74
Environmental, social and governance (ESG), 37
Environmental sustainability, 40–42, 74, 119, 127, 143

Erasmus Sustainability Hub, 24
Erasmus University Rotterdam
 (EUR), 23–25, 43, 126, 141
 iWill campaign, 24
Ethics, 38–40, 119, 127
External stakeholders, 13, 17, 18, 28,
 68, 91, 97, 121
 corporate partners, 79–82
 ecological environment, 84
 government, 82–83
 philanthropic partners, 83–84
EY, 10, 25

Financial capital, 61
Financial Times, 23
Firth, Verity, 90
Four Ds Model, 108
Fundraising, 45, 53, 83–84

Gallup, 26, 77
García, Juliet Villarreal, 62, 70, 97
Gender equity/equality, 15, 38, 42–43,
 104, 125–126
Gen Z and Y, 28, 71–72, 75, 97–98
Georgetown University, 73
Godin, Seth, 98
Golden Circle, 15, 47
Good Purpose study, 29
Gothenburg School of Business,
 Economics and Law, 44
Government, external stakeholders,
 82–83, 140
Graduate attributes, 74–75, 126
Greenleaf, Robert, 58
Green Mountain College, 41–42
Green Office, 24, 74
Gutmann, Amy, 39–40, 53–54, 59

Harvard Business Review, 25, 27, 28,
 113–114
Harvard Business School, 27
Harvard University, 37, 72, 124
Hebrew University, 2
Henderson, Rebecca, 27

Hesburgh, Theodore, Rev., 57
Hokkaido University's Graduate
 School of Infectious
 Diseases, 43
Humboldt University of Berlin, 18

IKEA, 98
Impact purpose, 4, 11, 14, 114
 defined, 12
 MBA of Value, 24
 multi-level benefits, 26
 organisational goal, 28
 rediscovering purpose, 123–124
Inclusion, Diversity, Equity and Access
 in a Learning community
 (IDEAL), 7–8
Informal leadership, 6, 54–55, 63, 119,
 128
Integrated purpose, 13–14
Internal stakeholders, 13, 17, 18, 28,
 68, 91, 97, 121
 academic staff, 75–77
 professional staff, 77–79
 students, 71–75
Ivy League, 53

Johnson & Johnson Credo, 13

Karolinska Institute, 18
Key performance indicators (KPIs),
 129
King's College, 95
KPMG International, 96
KU Leuven University, 18, 74,
 133–134
Kyoto University, 15, 18

Leadership
 conscious leadership, 60–61
 defined, 55
 goals and aspirations, 57
 purpose-driven leadership, 56–57
 servant leadership, 58–59
 shared leadership, 62–63

skills, 56
transformational leadership, 58
Leading impact, 128–129
LGBTQ+, 78, 98, 126
Logic models, 92–93

Mackey, John, 10, 40
Macquarie University, 50, 141
Macro-level benefits, 30–31
Martin V, Pope, 133
Massachusetts Institute of Technology (MIT), 13, 18
Massive Open Online Courses (MOOCs), 133–136
McKinsey Global Institute, 142
McNabb, Bill, 25
Meso-level benefits, 28–30
Micro-level benefits, 26–28
Millennials, 8, 28, 71–72, 75
Mindful learning, 135, 136
Mission, 9, 17–18
Mission statement, 4, 7, 17, 124
Monash University, 44
Morehouse College, 59
Mycoskie, Blake, 98

Net Impact, 74
Netherlands School of Economics, 23, 24
Netter Center, 54
Networked university, 137
Nooyi, Indra, 11
Northwestern University, 37
Not-for-profit organisations, 2, 73, 91, 143

Obama, Barack, 59
oikos International, 74
OpenCourseWare (OCW), 133
Optus, 141
Organisational change, 103–116, 119
 appreciative inquiry, 107–109
 defined, 106
 insights towards sustainability, 111–113
 Kotter's eight steps, 110–111
 stakeholder integration, 106
Organisational citizenship behaviour, 49, 63, 76–77
Organisational identity
 actions, 16
 mission, 16, 17–18
 philosophy and purpose, 16
 values, 16, 19–20
 vision, 16, 18
Organisational purpose, 12, 14
 defined, 10–11
Organisational theory, 106
Oxford University, 67–68, 79, 80
 Knowledge Exchange and Impact Team, 80

Patagonia, 3, 29
Peking University, 18
PepsiCo, 11
PERACH, tutoring project, 2
Personal purpose, defined, 9–10, 12
Pew Research Centre, 71–72
Philanthropic partners, 83–84
Philipps University, 142
Polman, Paul, 3, 11
Princeton University, 15, 54
Professional staff, 77–79
Pro-social behaviour
 companies, 3
 individuals, 2
Purpose at Work report, 29

Queensland University, 18
Quest University, 123, 138

Relational purpose, 13
Research Information Infrastructure project, 68
Research quality measurement exercises, 46
Richardson, Louise, 67

Role purpose, 10, 12
Rotterdam School of Management (RSM), 23–25

SDGs. *See* Sustainable Development Goals (SDGs)
SDSN. *See* Sustainable Development Solutions Network (SDSN)
Self-determination theory (SDT), 75–76
Self-enhancement values, 19
Self-transcended values, 19
Servant leadership, 58–59, 119
Service-learning, 73, 77, 126, 135
Shared leadership, 62–63
Signature story, 96–97
Simon Fraser University (SFU), 13, 35–36
Sinek, Simon, 8, 11, 15–16, 47
Sisodia, Raj, 10, 11, 40
Social capital, 61
Social change. *See also* Organisational change, 3
Social engagement, 14
Social immobility, 9
Social impact, 13, 15, 89–101, 119
　assessment tools, 92
　defined, 92
　logic models, 92–93
　measurement guide, 94–95
Social Impact Measurement Toolbox, 90–91
Social inclusion, 78, 83
Social innovation, 3, 8, 36, 126
Social justice, 13, 89, 90
Social learning, 109
Social marketing, 98
Social responsibility. *See also* Corporate social responsibility (CSR), 79, 127, 143
Societal purpose, 11–12
Society for Human Resource Management, 28

Spiritual capital, 61
Spiritual intelligence (SQ), 60–61, 63, 75
Stakeholder groups, 140–141
Stakeholder integration approach, 70, 106, 107, 119, 121, 126–127, 140–141
Stakeholder theory, 68, 119, 120
　university stakeholders' map, 70, 71
Stanford Social Innovation Review, 126, 138
Stanford University, 3, 18, 115, 124, 136
　The Alternative Breaks @ Stanford Program, 8
　Stanford Center on Poverty and Inequality, 8
State of the World Volunteerism Report, 2
Storytelling, 96
　risk mitigation, 99–100
　sharing, 129–130
Students
　bodies, 73–74
　-centered higher education, 136–137
　employability, 137
　internal stakeholders, 69–71, 71–73
　sustainability, 74
　volunteering, 73, 126
Sustainable Development Goals (SDGs), 3, 36, 42–45, 83, 84, 104
　teaching, 125
Sustainable Development Solutions Network (SDSN), 43
Sustainable universities, 40–42
　carbon-neutral, 40
　defined, 41
　sustainable development goals (SDGs), 42–45
　teaching curriculum, 41

TED, 15, 56, 62
Tessier-Lavigne, Marc, 7

Thomson Reuters, 133
Times Higher Education (THE), 23, 44, 104
TOMS Shoes, 98–99
Tony Chocolonely, 11
Transformational leadership, 58, 119

UC San Diego, 20
Unilever, 3, 11
'Universities are', Google search results, 1, 2, 147
University–industry collaboration model, 80–82
University leadership. *See also* Leadership, 115, 119
  formal and informal, 54–55
  management, 55
  vision, 57
University of Auckland, 3, 44, 103–105
University of Bath, 47
University of British Columbia, 140
University of California, 13, 18
University of Canterbury, 42
University of Copenhagen, 41
University of Edinburgh, 14
University of Gothenburg, 44
University of Hong Kong, 18
University of Lausanne, 42
University of Melbourne, 15, 136
University of Michigan, 37, 114
University of New South Wales, 111
University of New Zealand, 103
University of Northern British Columbia, 42
University of Notre Dame, 57

University of Oslo, 42
University of Pennsylvania (Penn), 39, 53
University of Southern California (USC), 17–18
University of Technology Sydney (UTS), 3, 13, 77
  appreciative inquiry, 109
  Social Impact Framework, 89–90
  Social Impact Measurement Toolbox, 90–91
  social justice, 90
  vision and strategy, 89
University of Texas, 30, 62, 97
University of Utah, 135
University of Zurich, 18

Values, 16, 19–20
  congruence, 14, 19, 27
  enacted, 19
  espoused, 19
Vision, 16, 18
Volunteering, 2, 8, 30–31, 37–38, 49, 54, 59, 73, 111, 114, 126

Wageningen University & Research (WUR), 140
Weaving connections, 122–123
Western Sydney University, 29, 95
Wholefood Markets, 40
Workplace inclusion, 78

Zander, Benjamin, 56
Zuckerberg, Mark, 72

www.ingramcontent.com/pod-product-compliance
Lightning Source LLC
Chambersburg PA
CBHW052052220426
43663CB00012B/2534